How to **HELP** a Hedgehog and **PROTECT** a Polar Bear

70 simple things YOU can do for our planet!

For my mum, Lynne, who taught me to care for the world and all its inhabitants. And for Fenya, with whom I cannot wait to share that love.
— J. F.

For Jayden, my family and all creatures great and small — especially those with small hands and a love for drawing!
— A. K.

How to use this book:

Hedgehog

20–30 cm

300 g

Look out for these size icons to find out approximately how big each animal is.

Only endangered animals are labelled in the habitat scenes, but there are many more to spot!

These weight icons show approximately how heavy each animal is.

First published 2018 by Nosy Crow Ltd
The Crow's Nest, 14 Baden Place,
Crosby Row, London, SE1 1YW
www.nosycrow.com

ISBN 978 1 78800 257 8

Text © Jess French 2018
Illustrations © Angela Keoghan 2018

The right of Jess French to be identified as the author and Angela Keoghan
to be identified as the illustrator of this work has been asserted.

A CIP catalogue record for this book is available from the British Library.

Printed in China.
Papers used by Nosy Crow are made from wood
grown in sustainable forests.

1 3 5 7 9 8 6 4 2

Contents

Introduction

Saving the planet might sound like an impossible job, but it's not too late for you to make a change. From creating hedgehog tunnels in your own back garden, to switching off lights when you leave a room to help protect the polar bears in the Arctic, there are plenty of little things you can do to make a big difference. It's difficult for animals to survive in the wild, but, as humans, we sometimes make it even harder.

Around the world, every second, we cut down enough trees to fill two football fields, destroying natural habitats to make room for our towns and cities. This is called deforestation and means that hundreds of animals lose their homes, or worse, are killed. Some of these forests are home to animals that are not found anywhere else on the planet. If we don't help now, those animals will become endangered and may be lost forever. And it's not just the forests that are affected; all over the world different kinds of habitat are damaged by the way we live our lives.

But don't worry, we know more now about how to protect our planet than we ever have done before. We're constantly discovering new ways to be more environmentally friendly and this will help make things better for the future. Even on a small scale, there are many things you can do to help save the world's most endangered animals and their habitats.

Taking care of nature is not just important, it's really fun too! So, what are you waiting for? Get outside, explore, and read on to discover how YOU can help protect our planet . . .

What is a habitat?

A habitat is a home for nature. Here are some of the major habitats in the world, all rich with wildlife.

GARDENS

A **garden** is an outside space near a house, which is part of a human home. Gardens often have pretty flowers and areas of green grass. Although gardens are not created naturally, they are still very important to wildlife.

HEDGEROWS

Hedgerows are long, thin stretches of bushy plants that were originally used by farmers to separate different fields. They are usually made up of woody shrubs, small trees and beautiful flowering plants. Some hedgerows contain prickly plants, like hawthorn, to stop sheep and cattle from leaving their fields.

HEATHLANDS

Heathlands are one of the rarest habitats in the world. They are wide, open spaces covered in low-lying plants, such as heather, grasses and gorse. They are usually found in places with very sandy or acidic soil. With their open areas for basking in the sun and healthy populations of insects, heathlands are just the right home for amphibians and reptiles.

WOODLANDS

Woodlands are areas of land that are covered by trees. Many are ancient habitats, and some trees are hundreds of years old! Woodland floors are littered with dead leaves and rotting wood, which makes a perfect environment for fungi, insects and shade-loving flowers.

HIGHLANDS

The Scottish **highlands** are made up of mountains, lochs and glens. 'Loch' is the Gaelic word for lake. The most famous loch is Loch Ness, where many people believe a monster called Nessie lives! A glen is a deep, narrow valley, which was carved by glaciers thousands of years ago during the last ice age.

WETLANDS

Wetlands are areas that are covered in water for all or most of the year. They are often created by flooding. Swamps, bogs, fens, marshes, mudflats and mangroves are all examples of wetlands.

FRESHWATER

Freshwater is water that contains very little salt. It is found in ponds, rivers, lakes and glaciers. Freshwater is much more rare than saltwater and it makes up less than three per cent of Earth's water!

COASTLINES

The **coastline** is the area where the land meets the sea. There are many different habitats along the coast, including beaches, sand dunes, estuaries and cliffs. All of these are salty, wet and home to lots of amazing animals.

OCEANS

Seas and **oceans** are enormous areas of saltwater. Over 70 per cent of the Earth's surface is covered by seas and oceans, making them the largest ecosystem in the world. They have the greatest variety of life, from enormous whales to tiny plankton, and from coral reefs in the warm tropics to polar bears in the freezing Arctic.

SAVANNAHS

Savannahs are huge, flat plains covered in long grasses and dotted with trees. They are usually found between rainforests and deserts. Savannahs are difficult environments to live in, so savannah animals depend upon one another to stay alive.

JUNGLES

Jungles are areas that are densely covered with trees and thick with tangled vegetation. They are usually found in tropical areas such as the Amazon in South America, the Daintree in Australia and the Congo in Africa. They are often wet and humid.

MOUNTAINS

A **mountain** is an area of land that reaches much higher than all of the land around it. It often has steep, rocky sides. Mountains are tough places to live, as there is not much food and it can be very cold. The higher you go up a mountain, the colder it gets!

Gardens

House sparrow

Garden tiger moth

Gardens are home to a lot of wild animals, including butterflies, hedgehogs, birds and even frogs and toads! As more and more houses are built, gardens are getting smaller and smaller.

Hedgehog

Small tortoiseshell
butterfly

These smaller gardens often have sturdy fences, or even walls, put up to separate them from their neighbours. This means animals like hedgehogs cannot pass freely from one garden to another, making it difficult for them to find food, water and mates.

Slow-worm

Garden species fact file

Hedgehog

A shy, nocturnal mammal who is often found snuffling and grunting around gardens. Hedgehogs mainly eat insects and they curl up into a spiny ball when they are frightened.

600 g

20–30 cm

Hedgehogs have been around for 15 million years!

0.5 g

48–52 mm

Small tortoiseshell butterfly

One of the first butterflies to appear in spring and often found hibernating in outbuildings over the winter months. Its caterpillars feed on stinging nettles.

How you can help

Plant native flowers with lots of nectar for bees and butterflies to visit.

Bees can see purple flowers more clearly than any other colour, whilst butterflies love them all!

Garden tiger moth

A big, brightly-coloured moth, whose markings warn that it is poisonous to predators. Its caterpillars are known as 'woolly bears' because they are very hairy!

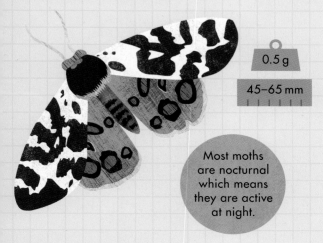

0.5 g

45–65 mm

Most moths are nocturnal which means they are active at night.

House sparrow

A small, brown bird with a dome-shaped skull. It has lived alongside humans for thousands of years and is often spotted nesting in the walls of buildings.

14–18 cm

24–40 g

Slow-worm

Often mistaken for a snake, it is actually a lizard with no legs! It likes to burrow and can usually be found hiding under rocks and logs.

100 g

Up to 50 cm

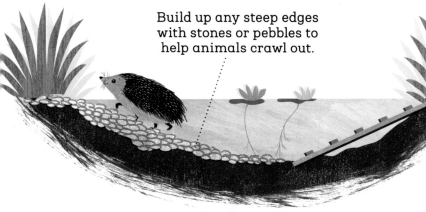

Build up any steep edges with stones or pebbles to help animals crawl out.

 If you have a pond in your garden, make sure there is a gentle slope so any creatures that fall in can easily escape.

 Collect rainwater in a large container, such as a water butt, and use that to water the plants in your garden.

 Don't put down slug pellets – they can kill hedgehogs and other garden animals.

 Cut a tunnel in your fence so hedgehogs can pass through your garden on their nightly food hunts.

Hedgerows

Cuckoo

Hedgerows are perfect homes for nectar-loving insects such as butterflies and moths and for farmland birds, dormice and hedgehogs, which nest in their dense leaves. Hedgerows make wildlife corridors, allowing animals to move safely from one place to another. They can also stop soil erosion and store carbon, which helps to combat climate change.

Hazel dormouse

Stag beetle

Turtle dove

Common lizard

Hedgerows are being cut down to make bigger fields, to be replaced with fences and to make space to build houses and other buildings. They are also threatened by the use of chemicals such as pesticides and fertilisers – bad news for all the animals that live here.

Hedgerow species fact file

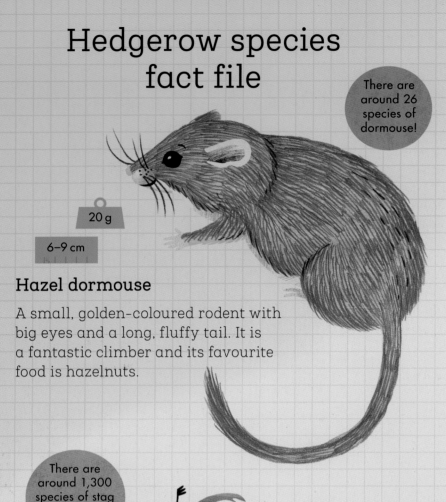

There are around 26 species of dormouse!

20 g

6–9 cm

Hazel dormouse

A small, golden-coloured rodent with big eyes and a long, fluffy tail. It is a fantastic climber and its favourite food is hazelnuts.

Attach nestboxes to trees for hazel dormice to snuggle up in during the day.

Unlike bird boxes, dormouse nestboxes have entrance holes facing the tree which reduces the chances that birds will try to use the box too.

There are around 1,300 species of stag beetle in the world!

Stag beetle

The adult male uses its big, antler-like jaws for fighting. Its young, called 'beetle grubs', live in old trees and rotting wood. They can take up to seven years to become adults.

5 cm   **3 g**

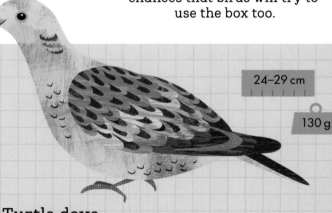

24–29 cm

130 g

Turtle dove

A small and dainty bird, best known for the soft purring noise it makes. It migrates to Africa in the winter months to escape the cold.

Cuckoo

A loud, grey bird with a stripy chest. It tricks other birds into raising its chicks by laying its eggs in their nests. Cheeky cuckoos!

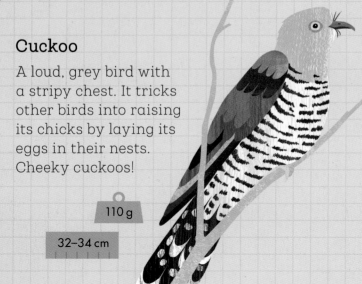

110 g

32–34 cm

Some lizards drop off their tails if they are caught by predators.

10–16 cm

5 g

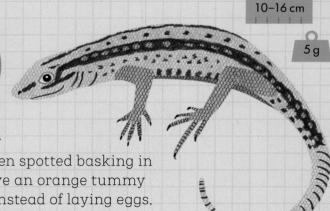

Common lizard

A brown lizard often spotted basking in the sun. Males have an orange tummy with black spots. Instead of laying eggs, the females give birth to live babies.

How you can help

 Take part in online nature surveys with the People's Trust for Endangered Species. In the 'Great Stag Hunt' you can look for stag beetles and record your sightings.

 Have fun exploring your local hedgerows to see what species you can spot. Perhaps there might be a chance for you and your family to grow a wildlife-friendly hedge in your own garden.

 Do what you can to spread the word at school. You could set up a club to care for local habitats or even invite an expert to teach you more about your favourite species.

 Leave out piles of logs so lizards can hibernate under them to stay warm and survive through the winter months.

A roof will keep everything dry!

Hollow stems, like bamboo canes, or holes drilled into wood, make good hiding spots for bees and ladybirds

Build insect hotels out of recycled wood to put in your local hedgerows.

Beetles, spiders and woodlice all love to hide between pine cones and twigs.

Heathlands

Heathlands support many rare species, such as the Dartford warbler, the nightjar, the woodlark and the ladybird spider. All six of the UK's reptile species can be found in heathlands.

Skylark

European hare

Wart-biter cricket

When new sites are targeted for development, heathland is often top of the list, as its dry soil has few nutrients and means it is no use to farmers. Over the last one hundred years, the UK has lost half of its heathland habitats.

Smooth snake

Shrill carder bumblebee

Heathland species fact file

Hares belong to a group of plant-eating mammals called lagomorphs.

European hare

A lightning-fast member of the rabbit family, it has long legs and black-tipped ears. It can often be seen bounding across fields in a zigzag pattern.

45–65 cm

3–4 kg

Shrill carder bumblebee

One of the smallest and rarest bumblebees, with dark stripes on a greyish-green body. When it flies it makes a very high-pitched buzz. Bees help pollinate crops so fewer bees is bad news for all of us.

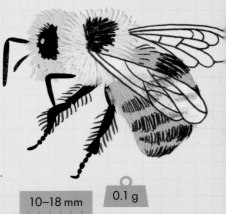

10–18 mm

0.1 g

Smooth snake

A grey-brown, spotted snake with a slender body and a small head. Very secretive and well camouflaged in heathland, it is mainly found in dry and sandy sites.

90–150 g

50–60 cm

Skylark

A streaky brown bird with a tuft of feathers on top of its head, known for its beautiful song. When the male sings, it flies straight up in the air, high into the sky.

Birds can eat 80 per cent of their own body weight in one day!

18–19 cm

35–45 g

Crickets are in the same family as grasshoppers.

31–37 mm

0.5 g

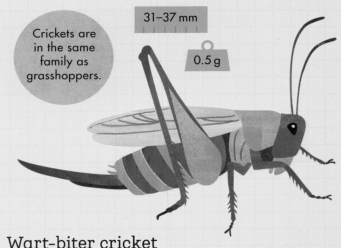

Wart-biter cricket

A large, green bush cricket with powerful back legs. It makes a clicking sound by rubbing its wings together. In the 1700s, people used them to bite warts off their skin!

How you can help

If it's not far, don't use the car. More cars means more air pollution, which is unhealthy for animals and people.

Keep dogs on a lead when you are walking in heathlands so that they don't scare birds that nest on the ground.

 Buy recycled paper and wood products, such as toilet roll, to save cutting down trees in heathland areas.

 Ask your grown-ups not to use chemical pesticides or fertilisers on flowers as these can kill bees.

 Pack a no-rubbish lunch. If rubbish is left on the ground or blows away, it can be really harmful to wildlife if they swallow it or get stuck in it.

About one third of all the rubbish we throw away is packaging, so use a lunchbox with dividers to keep your food fresh instead.

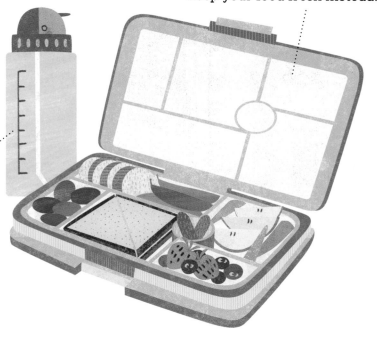

Choose a reusable bottle for your drinks.

Woodlands

Barbastelle bat

Red squirrel

Cicada

Woods and trees are home to more wildlife than any other habitat – and they have been around for thousands of years. Woodlands are especially important for beetles, woodland birds, mosses, ferns and lichens. Many mammals also depend on woodlands for food and places to hide.

Cosnard's
net-winged
beetle

Blue ground
beetle

Woodlands are rapidly shrinking
in size. They are threatened by
pollution, pests, disease and clearing
for new developments. Trees are
cut down to make space for new
housing, train lines and farmland.

Woodland species fact file

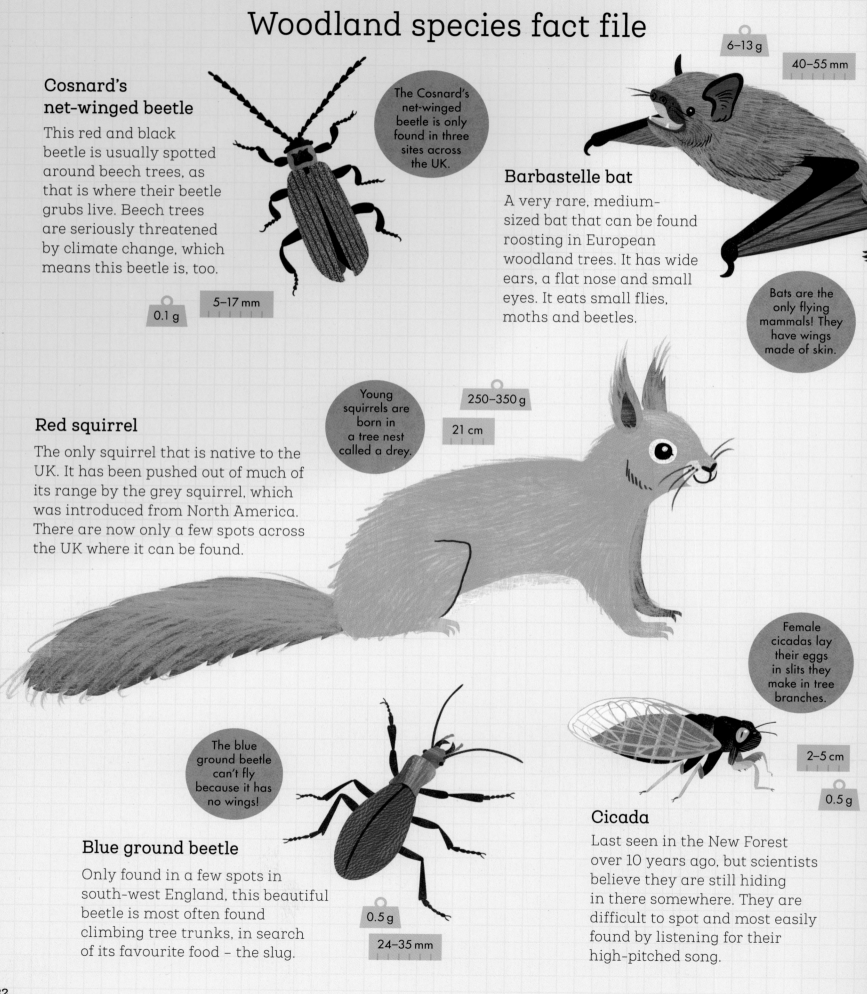

Cosnard's net-winged beetle

This red and black beetle is usually spotted around beech trees, as that is where their beetle grubs live. Beech trees are seriously threatened by climate change, which means this beetle is, too.

The Cosnard's net-winged beetle is only found in three sites across the UK.

0.1 g

5–17 mm

Barbastelle bat

6–13 g

40–55 mm

A very rare, medium-sized bat that can be found roosting in European woodland trees. It has wide ears, a flat nose and small eyes. It eats small flies, moths and beetles.

Bats are the only flying mammals! They have wings made of skin.

Red squirrel

The only squirrel that is native to the UK. It has been pushed out of much of its range by the grey squirrel, which was introduced from North America. There are now only a few spots across the UK where it can be found.

Young squirrels are born in a tree nest called a drey.

250–350 g

21 cm

Female cicadas lay their eggs in slits they make in tree branches.

2–5 cm

0.5 g

Blue ground beetle

The blue ground beetle can't fly because it has no wings!

Only found in a few spots in south-west England, this beautiful beetle is most often found climbing tree trunks, in search of its favourite food – the slug.

0.5 g

24–35 mm

Cicada

Last seen in the New Forest over 10 years ago, but scientists believe they are still hiding in there somewhere. They are difficult to spot and most easily found by listening for their high-pitched song.

How you can help

 Trees provide a warm and cosy habitat for tiny insects so don't pull bark or branches off of them.

 A log pile makes a wonderful habitat for all sorts of creatures so if you disturb one, don't forget to put it back how you found it.

 Adopt a red squirrel from The Wildlife Trust. By donating money each month, you can stop them from dying out.

 Save paper by using the same piece on both sides. The less paper you use, the less trees will need to be chopped down.

During the winter, many insects stay warm and cosy under logs.

 Download apps that help you monitor wildlife, such as the New Forest Cicada app which helps you search for cicadas if you're visiting the New Forest.

 Visit your local woodlands to learn about the species that live there. Search online to find accessible routes for wheelchairs, pushchairs and mobility aids.

Highlands

The Highlands are home for dragonflies and damselflies, which are common around the lochs. Red deer, beavers and eagles can also be found in the moors, rivers and skies.

Western capercaillie

Tiger worm

Golden eagle

Scottish wildcat

Climate change is one of the biggest threats to the Scottish highlands.
A change in temperature and rainfall may mean that some highland
species are no longer able to survive. It will also encourage new species
to spread to the area, bringing diseases that could kill highland animals.

Wetlands

Wetlands are very special ecosystems and they are home to many unique species. Reptiles, amphibians, invertebrates, mammals and birds can all be found in wetlands.

Grass snake

Norfolk
hawker

Green tansy beetle

European otter

Wetlands are drained for two reasons; firstly to provide dry land for developers to build on, and secondly to provide farmers with water to use on their crops, or land for them to graze their animals on. Draining destroys the wetland habitat. For the wetlands that are left, the main threats are pollution and the introduction of foreign species like killer shrimp, which kill off native animals.

Water vole

Wetland species fact file

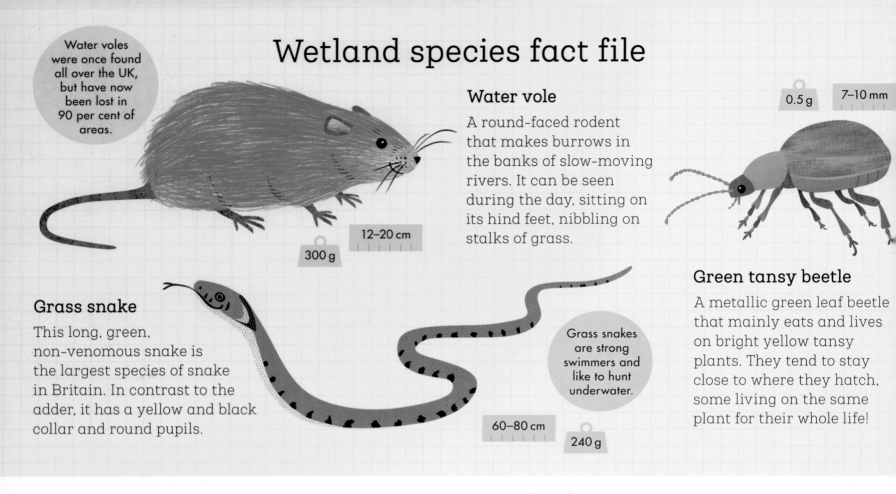

Water voles were once found all over the UK, but have now been lost in 90 per cent of areas.

Water vole

A round-faced rodent that makes burrows in the banks of slow-moving rivers. It can be seen during the day, sitting on its hind feet, nibbling on stalks of grass.

300 g

12–20 cm

0.5 g

7–10 mm

Green tansy beetle

A metallic green leaf beetle that mainly eats and lives on bright yellow tansy plants. They tend to stay close to where they hatch, some living on the same plant for their whole life!

Grass snake

This long, green, non-venomous snake is the largest species of snake in Britain. In contrast to the adder, it has a yellow and black collar and round pupils.

Grass snakes are strong swimmers and like to hunt underwater.

60–80 cm

240 g

How you can help

Stay on tracks and paths so you don't disturb nests on the ground.

Birds build nests to provide a safe place for eggs and young birds to grow.

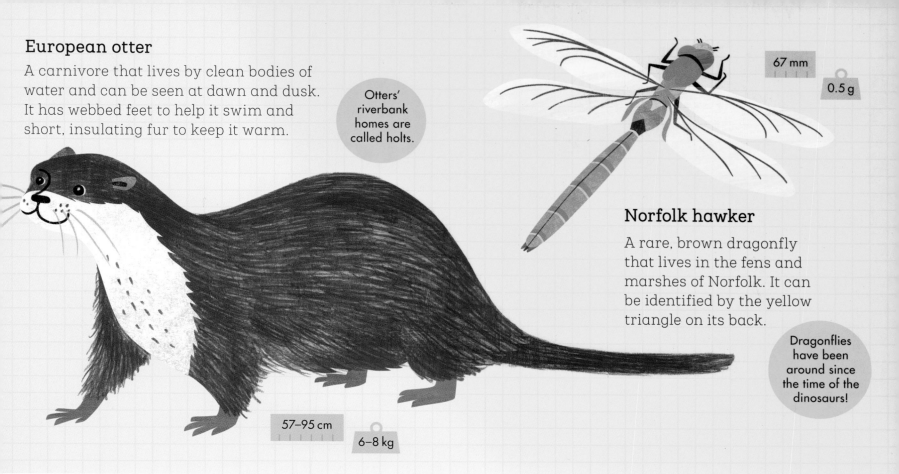

European otter

A carnivore that lives by clean bodies of water and can be seen at dawn and dusk. It has webbed feet to help it swim and short, insulating fur to keep it warm.

Otters' riverbank homes are called holts.

57–95 cm

6–8 kg

67 mm

0.5 g

Norfolk hawker

A rare, brown dragonfly that lives in the fens and marshes of Norfolk. It can be identified by the yellow triangle on its back.

Dragonflies have been around since the time of the dinosaurs!

Join in with riverbank restoration programs to help protect the habitat for river wildlife.

Take part in online dragonfly and butterfly counts to find out which species live in your local wetland.

Learn to identify wetland species and tell your family and friends about why they are so important.

Volunteer to monitor a local water vole population.

Water voles are Britain's fastest declining wild mammal. Look out for their burrows in the riverbank, often with nibbled grass around the entrance.

Freshwater

Much like hedgerows act as corridors for land animals, rivers and streams help freshwater species to move safely around wetland ecosystems. These bodies of freshwater are home to fish such as eels, pike and roach, mammals like water voles and otters and beautiful birds such as kingfishers.

White-clawed crayfish

Freshwater habitats suffer from pollution from many different sources. Industrial sites, sewage tanks and fish farms all pump their waste into freshwater habitats. Fertilisers that drain off farmland into freshwater can cause algae and weeds to grow too much, choking the water and killing off all other species that are living in the area.

Great crested newt

Vendace

Freshwater pearl mussel

Amazon river dolphin

Freshwater species fact file

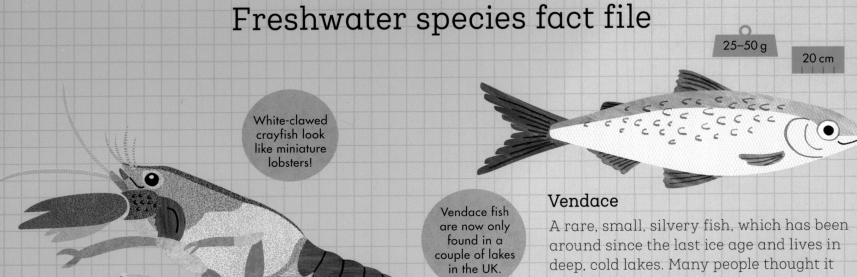

25–50 g

20 cm

Vendace

A rare, small, silvery fish, which has been around since the last ice age and lives in deep, cold lakes. Many people thought it had already gone extinct.

White-clawed crayfish look like miniature lobsters!

Vendace fish are now only found in a couple of lakes in the UK.

90 g

12 cm

White-clawed crayfish

The only species of freshwater crayfish that is native to the British Isles, it is endangered by the introduction of non-native species like the American signal crayfish.

20 g

12–15 cm

Freshwater pearl mussels cling on to the gills of salmon when they are first born.

Freshwater pearl mussel

Large, dark brown mussels that can live for more than 100 years! They live on the bottom of riverbeds, where they filter food out of the water.

Dolphins communicate using a variety of clicks and whistles.

100–160 kg

2–3 m

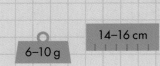

Amazon river dolphin

A mammal that lives in South American rivers. It has a long, thin snout, small eyes and a grey-pink body. It eats a variety of river fish, including ferocious piranhas.

Amphibians bask in the sun to keep warm.

6–10 g

14–16 cm

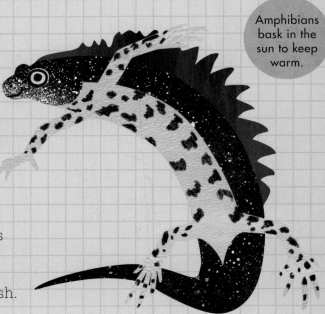

Great crested newt

A warty brown amphibian with a jagged crest along its back and a bright orange tummy. It prefers big ponds with lots of weeds and no fish.

How you can help

 Be responsible and put rubbish in the bin. If you drop it on the ground, it might be washed into a river and could harm freshwater wildlife.

 Ask your grown-up not to use chemical pesticides and fertilisers in the garden – they can run into rivers and could kill the fish.

Use biodegradable cleaning products, which will not pollute waterways such as rivers and streams.

Look for great crested newts with your friends. Any ponds that they are living in are protected by law, which means you are not allowed to disturb them or damange their habitat.

The great crested newt is one of three newts found in the British Isles, along with the smooth newt and the palmate newt. It is the biggest and least common of the three.

Coastlines

Little tern

Coasts are home to seabirds, waders, sea mammals and lots of other creatures, too. They soak up energy from the sea and help stop the risk of flooding and erosion. It is important to protect coasts, not only for animals, but for people, too.

Natterjack toad

Harbour
porpoise

Puffin

The greatest threat to coastal species is the litter
that is washed up by the tides. Plastic litter is often
found in the stomachs of dead sea creatures,
and sometimes it strangles them when it gets
wrapped around their bodies. Coasts are also
threatened by pollution from farming,
industrial waste and sewage.

Sand lizard

Coastal species fact file

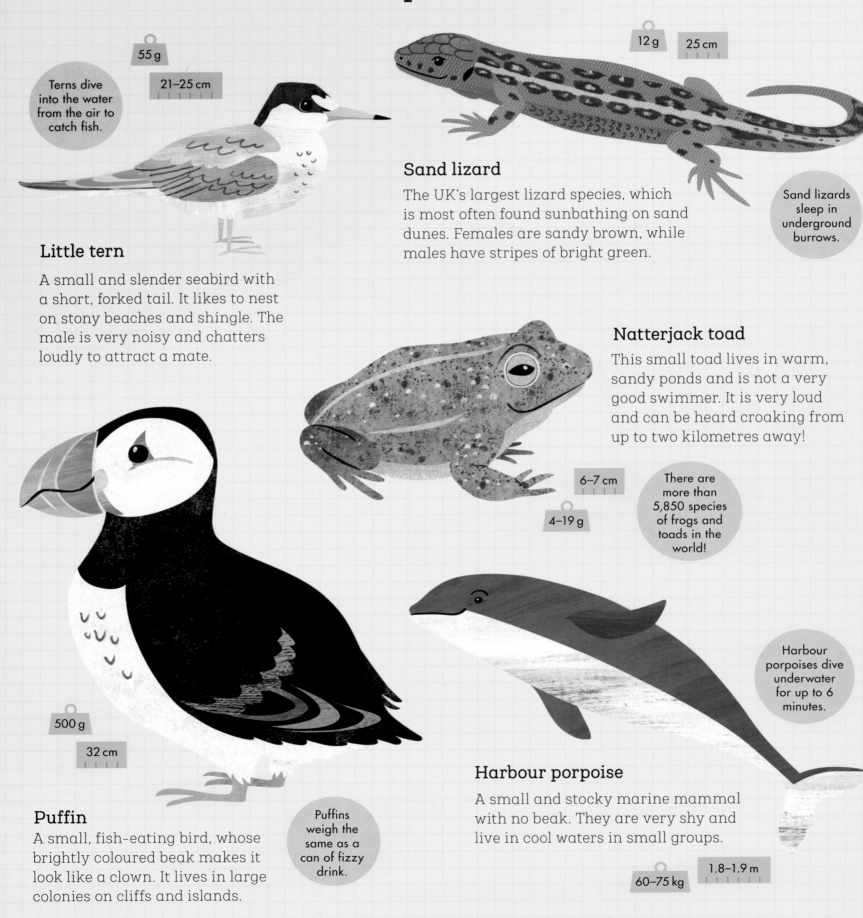

55 g

21–25 cm

Terns dive into the water from the air to catch fish.

12 g

25 cm

Sand lizard

The UK's largest lizard species, which is most often found sunbathing on sand dunes. Females are sandy brown, while males have stripes of bright green.

Sand lizards sleep in underground burrows.

Little tern

A small and slender seabird with a short, forked tail. It likes to nest on stony beaches and shingle. The male is very noisy and chatters loudly to attract a mate.

Natterjack toad

This small toad lives in warm, sandy ponds and is not a very good swimmer. It is very loud and can be heard croaking from up to two kilometres away!

6–7 cm

4–19 g

There are more than 5,850 species of frogs and toads in the world!

Harbour porpoises dive underwater for up to 6 minutes.

500 g

32 cm

Puffin

A small, fish-eating bird, whose brightly coloured beak makes it look like a clown. It lives in large colonies on cliffs and islands.

Puffins weigh the same as a can of fizzy drink.

Harbour porpoise

A small and stocky marine mammal with no beak. They are very shy and live in cool waters in small groups.

1.8–1.9 m

60–75 kg

How you can help

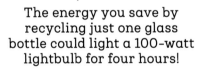

The energy you save by recycling just one glass bottle could light a 100-watt lightbulb for four hours!

 Join in with a litter-pick on a local beach.

 Use a reusable water bottle when you go to the beach, instead of buying a new plastic one.

 Use unbleached paper, as bleach can damage water systems.

 To save water and keep our coasts healthy, don't leave the tap running when you brush your teeth.

 Pick up your dog's poo when you take it for a walk, so it doesn't spread disease.

 Don't release sky lanterns or balloons. When they land, wildlife such as coastal birds and fish can get tangled in them or choke on them.

Oceans

Oceans contain many weird and wonderful creatures, from octopuses and dolphins to seahorses and starfishes, also known as sea stars. They are also home to the largest animal in the world, the blue whale.

Leatherback turtle

Polar bear

Blue whale

Fishing is a big problem for oceans. If too many adult fish are caught then there will be no babies to grow up into the next generation. And it is not only the fish that suffer from fishing. Animals like turtles, dolphins and whales die when they get tangled in fishing nets. This is called 'bycatch'. Our litter also causes huge problems for oceans. If things don't change, the ocean will soon contain more plastic than fish.

Atlantic bluefin tuna

Coral

Ocean species fact file

150–450 kg

2.4–3 m

270–360 kg

One in every 1,000 turtle hatchlings makes it to adulthood.

1.8–2.2 m

Polar bears can smell seals from over a kilometre away!

Leatherback turtle

A huge marine turtle with a leathery shell and long, strong flippers. Its favourite food is jellyfish.

Polar bear

A huge bear with thick white fur, which keeps it insulated in the freezing Arctic Circle. It usually lives alone and feeds almost exclusively on seals.

Atlantic bluefin tuna

An enormous, torpedo-shaped, lightning-fast fish. It can swim for thousands of miles and dive to more than 1,000 metres.

Coral reefs are sometimes called 'rainforests of the sea'.

Coral

A very important organism found in oceans, made up of colonies of tiny creatures called 'polyps'. Over a long time, it grows into a coral reef, which is home to a vast number of fish and sea creatures.

Bluefin tuna can live up to 40 years!

2–2.5 m

250 kg

180,000 kg

30 m

Blue whale

The largest animal ever known to have existed, measuring around 30 metres long, its heart is as big as a small car!

Blue whales usually travel alone or in small groups.

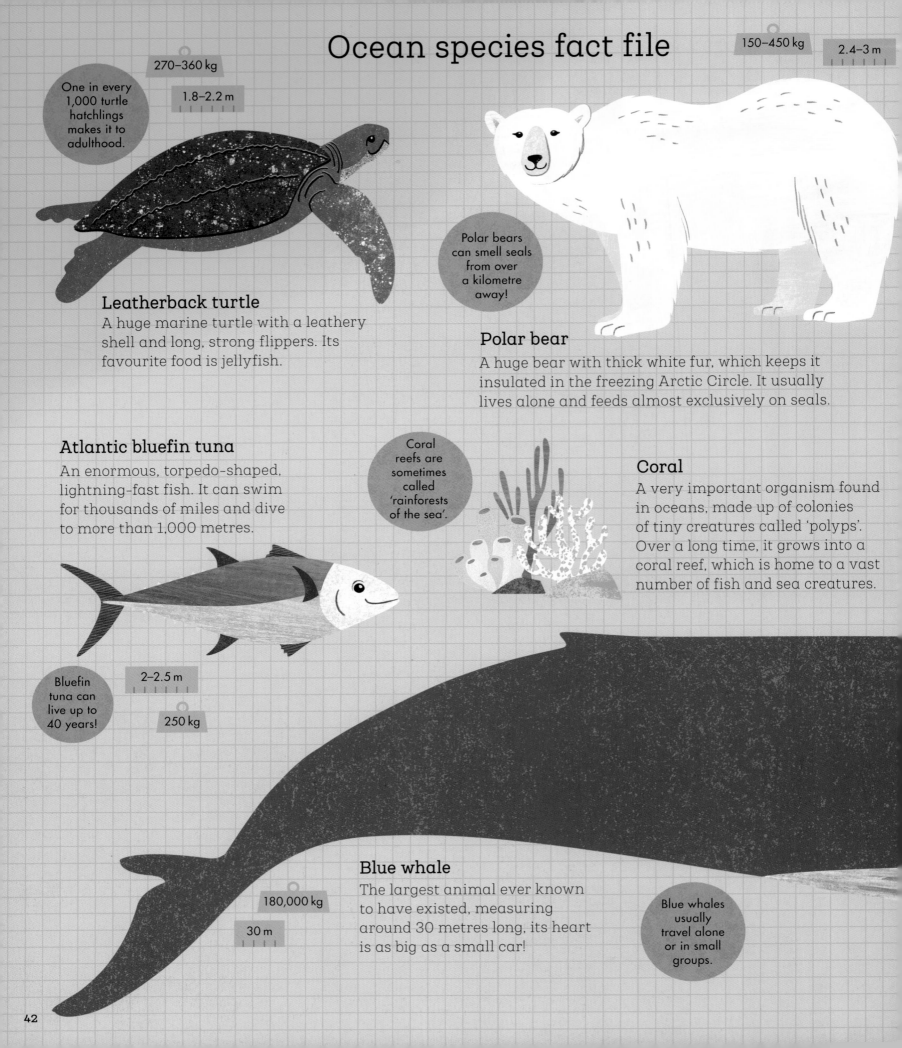

How you can help

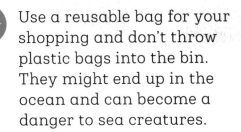

 Use a reusable bag for your shopping and don't throw plastic bags into the bin. They might end up in the ocean and can become a danger to sea creatures.

Only buy responsibly and sustainably sourced fish to eat to prevent over-fishing of endangered species.

 Don't buy wild-caught fish as pets – if we continue to take animals from the wild there will eventually be none left.

Plastic bags and other plastic rubbish thrown into the ocean kill more than one million sea creatures every year!

 Never flush wet wipes down the toilet – they don't break down like toilet paper and can harm animals in the ocean.

 Don't use plastic straws to drink through. If you really need a straw, use a metal or paper one.

Savannahs

Rothschild's
giraffe

There are savannahs all over the world. Africa's savannahs
support zebras, giraffes and lions. In Australian savannahs
you could find kangaroos, wallabies and echidnas. Brazil's
savannahs are home to tapirs, jaguars and armadillos.

African wild dog

Ethiopian wolf

Black rhino

African cheetah

Deforestation and the building of mines threaten the savannah ecosystem, because there isn't enough room left for its animals who need lots of space. But the animals that live in the savannah are also targeted directly. Famous African animals are hunted and killed so that rich tourists can take their heads and skins home as trophies. Elephants are killed for their tusks, which poachers sell as ivory.

Savannah species fact file

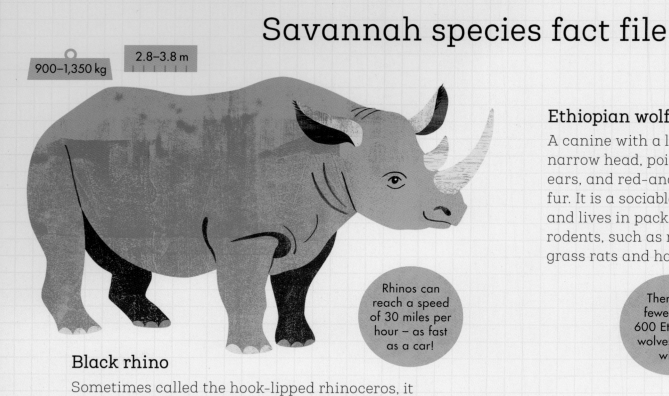

900–1,350 kg

2.8–3.8 m

Black rhino

Sometimes called the hook-lipped rhinoceros, it has a pointed upper lip, which helps it to pluck fruit and leaves from the branches of trees.

Rhinos can reach a speed of 30 miles per hour – as fast as a car!

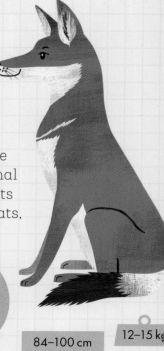

Ethiopian wolf

A canine with a long, narrow head, pointed ears, and red-and-white fur. It is a sociable animal and lives in packs. It eats rodents, such as mole rats, grass rats and hares.

There are fewer than 600 Ethiopian wolves in the wild.

84–100 cm

12–15 kg

Rothschild's giraffe

A light-coloured giraffe, which has no patches below its knees, so it looks like it's wearing long socks! Like all giraffes they have long necks, legs and tongues.

Giraffes can feed on leaves and buds at the very top of trees.

4.3–5.5 m

680–1,360 kg

Support organisations involved in savannah wildlife conservation by adopting an animal or doing a sponsored event.

ADOPT

WWF

WWF

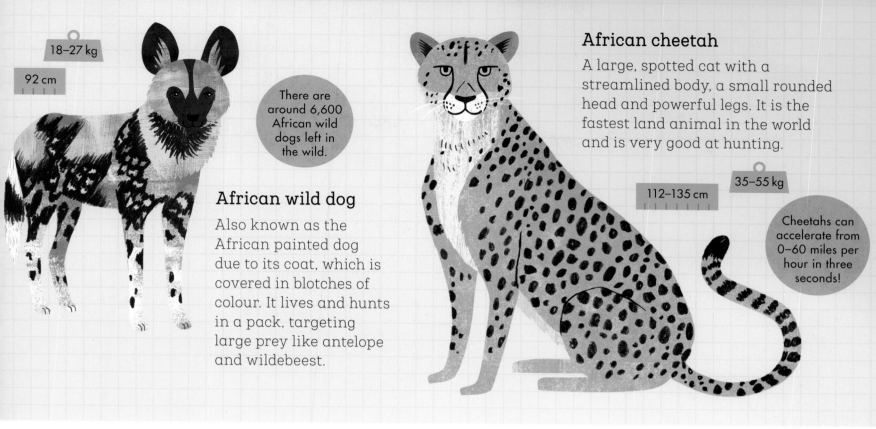

18–27 kg

92 cm

There are around 6,600 African wild dogs left in the wild.

African wild dog

Also known as the African painted dog due to its coat, which is covered in blotches of colour. It lives and hunts in a pack, targeting large prey like antelope and wildebeest.

African cheetah

A large, spotted cat with a streamlined body, a small rounded head and powerful legs. It is the fastest land animal in the world and is very good at hunting.

35–55 kg

112–135 cm

Cheetahs can accelerate from 0–60 miles per hour in three seconds!

How you can help

 Recycle old clothes and buy second-hand clothes. Making new clothes requires a lot of water and energy and the dyes and chemicals used in the process are damaging to the environment.

Use social media to share messages about how people can help.

 Never buy products made from animal parts, such as ivory. Savannah animals are poached for these products.

Coffee crops are often grown in elephants' habitats. If you buy coffee, make sure it is elephant-friendly. Look for the certified Fairtrade Mark on the packaging.

Have a 'rhino rant' – tell your friends and family about the plight of the rhino and why we should protect it.

Jungles

Jungles are filled with incredible species.
Brightly coloured birds and butterflies fill
the skies, whilst monkeys and snakes swing
and slither through the trees.

Orangutan

Clouded
leopard

Proboscis
monkey

Asian elephant

Tiger

Jungles are disappearing at a terrifying rate.
They are cut down to make space to graze cattle,
to use the trees for wood for building houses and
furniture, and to plant crops such as palm trees
to make palm oil, which is used in cooking and
found in many kinds of foods.

Jungle species fact file

The proboscis monkey's nose acts as loudspeaker for his call.

Proboscis monkey

A strange-looking monkey from Borneo, named because of its enormous nose. It usually lives around swamplands and is a very good swimmer.

53–62 cm

7–22 kg

Orangutan

An intelligent and gentle Asian ape. They are incredible climbers and spend almost all of their time in the treetops. There are two species, the Bornean orangutan and the Sumatran orangutan.

45–100 kg   1.2–1.4 m

Orangutans have declined by around 50 per cent in the last 60 years.

2–4 m

90–300 kg

There are now just 4,000 tigers left in the wild.

Tiger

The largest member of the cat family, famous for its orange and black stripes, which provide it with camouflage. It comes out mainly at night to hunt pigs, deer, buffalo and antelope.

11–30 kg

84 cm

Clouded leopard

A very secretive cat, which skulks through dense jungle in silence, climbing trees with ease and grace. It is found across Southeast Asia and throughout the Himalayas.

Elephants can live up to around 70 years!

Asian elephant

Smaller than the African elephant, but still one of the largest land animals on the planet. It has huge ears and an amazing long trunk, which it uses for breathing, smelling, trumpeting, drinking, communicating and even picking things up!

5.5–6.5 m   2,000–4,900 kg

How you can help

Only buy products that contain sustainably sourced palm oil. To create palm oil, an area of rainforest the size of 300 football pitches has to be chopped down each hour!

'Eco' products tend to cost more, but if we all keep buying them, the prices should go down.

Put a 'No Junk Mail' sign on your door to reduce how much paper you waste.

Wear an extra layer on cold days rather than turning the heating up.

To reduce the number of jungle trees that need to be cut down, don't print things out if you don't need to.

About 40 per cent of the energy we use at home is for heat. And half of that is wasted!

Learn about which companies clear rainforests to make their products and avoid buying from them. Only buy wood that is certified by the FSC. This means it has been grown from a well-managed forest.

Mountains

Red panda

Mountain gorilla

Mountain species often have thick, woolly coats to keep them warm. Some mountain animals have specially designed feet, to keep their balance on the rocky mountainsides. Even the plants in mountain areas are specially adapted to keep them out of the wind.

Chinchilla

When new mountain roads are built, they allow loggers, poachers and miners to travel to areas that are normally very difficult to get to. New roads can also cause erosion to the steep mountain edges. Some mountain habitats are also being destroyed by the human wars that are taking place on their slopes.

Snow leopard

Mountain species fact file

90–180 kg

1.2–1.8 m

There are only around 880 mountain gorillas left in the wild.

4–6.5 kg

58 cm

Red panda

A cat-sized mammal that is more closely related to weasels and raccoons than the black and white giant panda. It lives in mountainous forests and feeds mainly on bamboo, eggs, flowers and berries.

Red pandas communicate by making a twittering sound.

Mountain gorilla

An enormous black ape with long, shaggy hair that is closely related to humans. They live in groups of many females and young with one adult male, called the silverback.

Chinchillas usually live in herds of 100 or more.

370–490 g

30 cm

Chinchilla

A South American rodent with soft and silky fur and a long, bushy tail. Found in the Andes mountain range of Chile and hunted for its fur.

Snow leopards have long furry tails that help them to balance.

Snow leopard

One of the most mysterious cats in the world, it lives in the remote mountains of Central Asia. Even its big feet are covered in thick hair to keep them warm.

1.1 m

27–55 kg

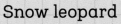

How you can help

 If something breaks, instead of buying something new, which will require materials and energy – learn how to fix it.

Make your own eco-friendly party decorations instead of using balloons to reduce plastic waste.

Create flyers to share with neighbours telling them how they can help, too.

Use energy-efficient light bulbs as they use much less electricity than conventional bulbs.

Make sure your flyers are made from recycled paper.

 Reuse envelopes when you can to stop so many mountain trees being chopped down.

 Never buy products made of real animal fur. Many mountain animals are killed just for their fur.

Monarch butterflies migrate from North America and southern Canada down to Mexico

Nightingales migrate from the UK to south-west Africa

Migrations

Some animals belong to more than one habitat, making long distance journeys every year in search of food or mates. This is called migration. All different kinds of animals – birds, fish, insects, mammals, reptiles and crustaceans – go on these incredible journeys.

Most migrant birds leave the UK in the winter when it starts to get cold, and return again in the summer. However, there are a few species, such as waxwings, which come to the UK in winter from even colder regions like Scandinavia.

For some migrant animals, with extremely long migrations, the UK might just be one stop along a very long journey!

Lapwings migrate from Scandinavia to the UK

Golden orioles migrate from Africa and Western Asia to the UK

Humpback whales migrate from polar waters to tropical waters

Climate change affects the plants that grow in different areas. This means that some migrant species arrive at their destinations expecting to find lots of food to eat – but nothing is there! Changing temperatures also confuse birds about when they should leave. Oil spills are another big problem for birds that have stopovers in contaminated areas along their journeys. Some migrants are even trapped by poachers or shot by hunters as they fly by.

Migrant species fact file

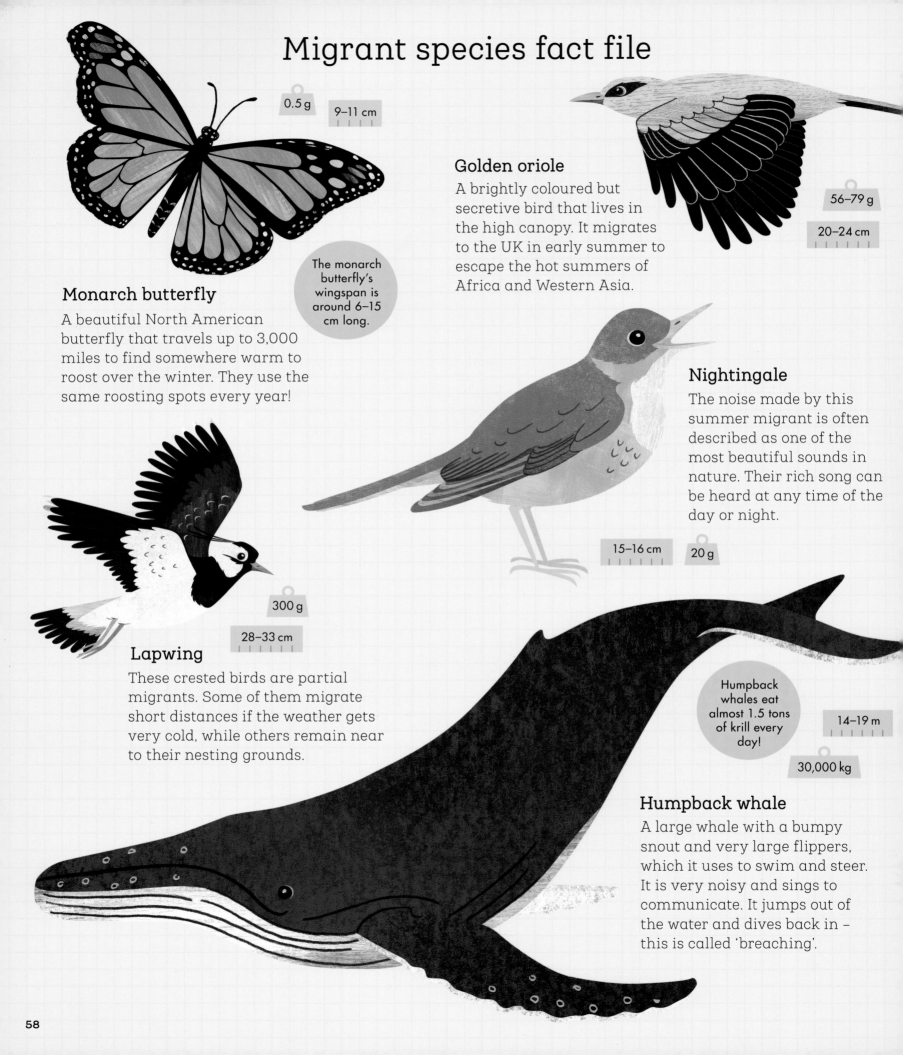

0.5 g   9–11 cm

Golden oriole

A brightly coloured but secretive bird that lives in the high canopy. It migrates to the UK in early summer to escape the hot summers of Africa and Western Asia.

56–79 g

20–24 cm

Monarch butterfly

A beautiful North American butterfly that travels up to 3,000 miles to find somewhere warm to roost over the winter. They use the same roosting spots every year!

The monarch butterfly's wingspan is around 6–15 cm long.

Nightingale

The noise made by this summer migrant is often described as one of the most beautiful sounds in nature. Their rich song can be heard at any time of the day or night.

15–16 cm   20 g

Lapwing

These crested birds are partial migrants. Some of them migrate short distances if the weather gets very cold, while others remain near to their nesting grounds.

300 g

28–33 cm

Humpback whales eat almost 1.5 tons of krill every day!

14–19 m

30,000 kg

Humpback whale

A large whale with a bumpy snout and very large flippers, which it uses to swim and steer. It is very noisy and sings to communicate. It jumps out of the water and dives back in – this is called 'breaching'.

How you can help

Attach window stickers to clear windows to stop birds accidentally flying into them.

If you see a baby bird on the ground, leave it alone. It's likely that its mummy will be nearby.

Put a bell on the collar of your cat so that it can't sneak up on birds.

Put food and water out for the birds, especially in winter.

Look out for wildlife campaigns and support the ones that matter to you, like The Big Garden Birdwatch by the RSPB.

Although bread is not harmful to birds, it doesn't provide many nutrients and can choke small chicks. Instead, put out chopped nuts in winter, and seeds and dried fruit in the summer.

Grow plants with berries for birds to eat.

Go birdwatching with friends and log all the different birds you can spot.

More about endangered species

So far, scientists have estimated that there are around 1.5 million different types of animal in the world, but there are likely to be many more. They are divided into six different groups and here are the approximate numbers of species for each one:

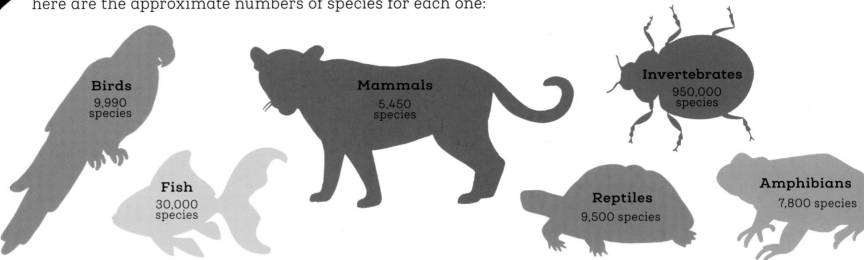

Birds 9,990 species

Fish 30,000 species

Mammals 5,450 species

Invertebrates 950,000 species

Reptiles 9,500 species

Amphibians 7,800 species

The IUCN (International Union for Conservation of Nature) is the world's main organisation for the conservation of animals from around the planet. They put together lists of animals, called Red Lists, which show the threatened status of species within a certain country or region. The endangered species are grouped into seven different categories, which show the risk that they will become extinct if we do not try to protect them. You can find out more and even look up the status of your favourite animal on their website: *www.iucnredlist.org*

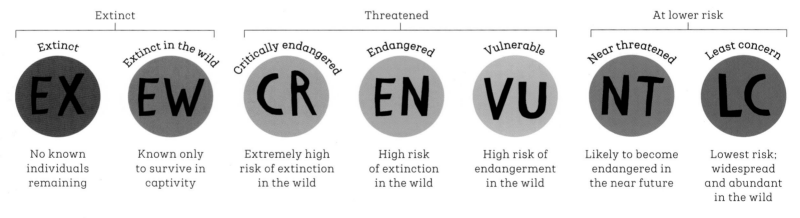

Extinct		Threatened			At lower risk	
Extinct EX	**Extinct in the wild** EW	**Critically endangered** CR	**Endangered** EN	**Vulnerable** VU	**Near threatened** NT	**Least concern** LC
No known individuals remaining	Known only to survive in captivity	Extremely high risk of extinction in the wild	High risk of extinction in the wild	High risk of endangerment in the wild	Likely to become endangered in the near future	Lowest risk; widespread and abundant in the wild

It is not only animals which can become endangered. There are six main habitats which are essential to life on our planet as they provide food, water, shelter and even the oxygen we breathe. All of these habitats are threatened by human actions, too.

Rainforest — Marine — Forest — Grassland — Desert — Polar

← Most animal species live here.

Least animal species live here. →

Although rainforests cover only a small part of the Earth, they're home to over half the world's plants and animals.

One and a half acres of rainforest are lost every second.

Rainforests once covered 14 per cent of the Earth's land surface.

Now they only cover 6 per cent.

Experts estimate that the last remaining rainforests could be destroyed in less than 40 years.

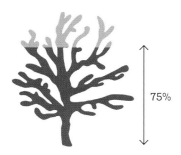

75%

Coral reefs are home to one quarter of the world's fish species and they protect the coastlines of 109 countries. But approximately 75 per cent of the world's coral reefs are rated as threatened.

About 50 per cent of all turtle species are threatened with extinction.

50%

Out of the six animal groups, amphibians are the most endangered. But, according to the IUCN, a number of species from every group are considered threatened too. Here are some approximate figures:

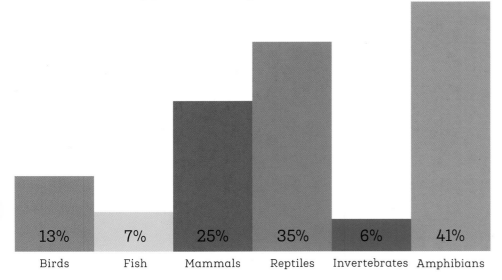

Birds	Fish	Mammals	Reptiles	Invertebrates	Amphibians
13%	7%	25%	35%	6%	41%

% of threatened species in each animal group

Going, going... gone

If we aren't careful, then animals that are endangered now will soon become extinct, like these amazing creatures who have already disappeared:

Dodo

Woolly mammoth

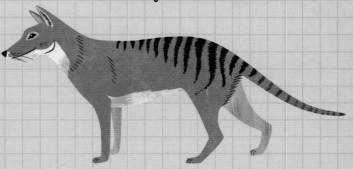

Tasmanian tiger

... and many, many more like the Pyrenean ibex, the passenger pigeon, the quagga, the Caribbean monk seal and the great auk.

More ways to help

Our beautiful planet is in danger. If we do not act soon, we will all be fighting for survival. But don't despair! If we are kind to the environment, it will give us everything we need for happy, healthy lives. We can change the future. We can save the planet. And the power to do it is in YOUR hands.

SAVE ENERGY

Only use things that run on electricity when you really need to and turn them off when you are finished. Using electricity burns up fossil fuels such as oil and coal, which is poisonous to the atmosphere.

RECYCLE

Recycle as much as you can! Cans, bottles, paper, cardboard, plastic and glass can all be turned into brand new products if they are recycled.

SPEAK OUT

Tell everyone you meet about the problems facing our planet and how we can fix them. We will all need to work together to solve the problems we have created.

SAVE WATER

Turn off the tap when you are not using the water. Creating clean drinking water uses lots of energy and produces pollution.

REUSE

Use things more than once! Before you throw something away, ask yourself how you could use it again.

REDUCE

Think before you buy! Reduce the amount of waste you produce by buying less in the first place. Also avoid buying things with lots of packaging.

PESTER POWER

Grown-ups often make most of the decisions about what to buy from the shops. Use your pester power to remind them to look for products that are friendly to the environment and don't have lots of packaging.

Glossary

Amphibian   A cold-blooded animal with a backbone, such as a newt or toad. Amphibians start their life with gills and a tail.

Camouflage   The way that an animal's colour or markings help it to blend in with its surroundings.

Climate change   A change in the Earth's temperature.

Compost   A rich soil made from dead plants and vegetables.

Conservation   Protecting animals, plants and the environment.

Deforestation   Clearing an area of trees.

Ecosystem   All of the plants and animals found in a certain area.

Environment   Everything around us including air, water, rocks and plants.

Erosion   The wearing away of soil and rock.

Extinct   When there are no more of a species left alive.

Fertiliser   A chemical or natural substance added to soil to make plants grow better.

Glacier   Thick ice that moves slowly downhill.

Habitat   The place where an animal or plant lives.

Hibernation   Sleeping through the cold winter months.

Industrial waste   Waste produced by places where humans work, such as factories.

Invertebrate   An animal without a backbone.

Mammal   A warm-blooded animal with a skeleton and fur or hair on its skin. Mammal mothers produce milk to feed their babies.

Mating   The way animals make babies.

Migration   Moving from one place to another, usually at a certain time of year.

Native   Belonging to or originally found in an area.

Organism   A living thing such as an animal or plant.

Pesticide   A substance used to kill pests.

Poach   To hunt or steal something that it is against the law to kill or take.

Pollution   Something in the soil, water or air that is harmful to plants and animals.

Reptile   A cold-blooded animal with a backbone, such as a snake or lizard. Reptiles are often covered in scales.

Restoration   Returning something to the way it used to be.

Sewage   Dirty water from toilets and drains.

Species   A group of plants and animals that are very similar and can breed with each other.

Sustainable   Something that we can carry on using or doing for a long time without it being used up.

Vegetation   Plant life.

Try searching for these online to find more ways you can help:

Go ladybird spotting with the UK Ladybird Survey

Hunt for sexton beetles with the National Silphidae Recording Scheme

Look out for oil beetles with Buglife

Watch out for weevils with the Weevil Recording Scheme

Look out for longhorn beetles with the Longhorn Recording Scheme

Hunt for grasshoppers with the Grasshopper and Related Species Recording Scheme

Sniff out dung beetles with DUMP! (the dung beetle UK mapping project)

Create a buzz with the Great British Bee Count

Index

INTRODUCTION

It is difficult to imagine a world without transport. Every day, people catch buses, ride bicycles, drive cars and catch trains. Transport brings us the daily newspaper and the post, and keeps the shops supplied with goods. This book charts the development of land and sea transport, from the earliest days to the vast changes seen in the 20th century.

Throughout history, most people never went more than a few kilometres from their homes. In the past, travel was difficult and unsafe. The development of the railways and the invention of the motor car have made our lives interesting and comfortable – and more dangerous. Steam trains and early motor cars were unclean and often highly unreliable. Today's vehicles are cleaner, safer and more comfortable than ever before.

Yet the vast increase in the numbers of cars and other vehicles in the second half of the 20th century has itself caused environmental problems. Now, engineers and planners are looking at ways to make transport even cleaner and more efficient.

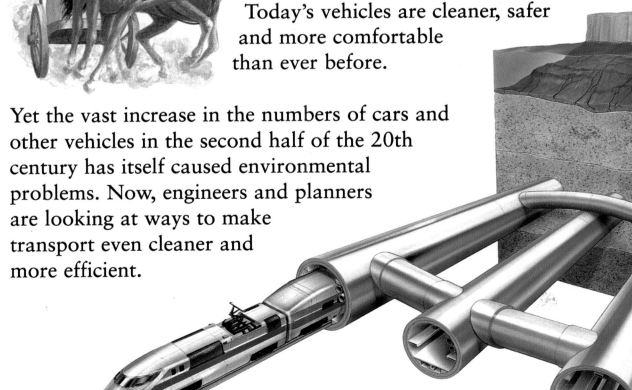

WHEEL POWER

The wheel is one of the most important inventions of all time. Imagine life without it – how difficult it would be to get around, and how heavy objects would have to be dragged or carried. The first wheels were used in Mesopotamia, part of modern Iraq, over 5,000 years ago. Tree trunks were probably used first as rollers for heavy loads, then sliced to make thinner, solid wheels. It was found that if spaces were left in the wood, creating spokes, wheels were much lighter. The use of wheels spread throughout Europe and, in the 16th century with the Spanish conquest, to America.

EARLY EVIDENCE
Archaeologists know what the first wheels looked like (*above*) from ancient mosaics found in the Middle East.

CHARIOTS
Four-wheeled chariots were first used by the Sumerian people of Mesopotamia in the Middle East in about 2500 BC. The ancient Romans used two-wheeled chariots (*left*) to travel about their huge empire. They were also the first people to build proper, hard-wearing roads.

MEDIEVAL MUDDLE
People in the Middle Ages rarely travelled far from their own villages (*below*). After the collapse of the Roman Empire, roads fell into disrepair, and were often so muddy that they could not be used. People and horses sometimes drowned in deep pot holes!

PANALPINA
5 Continents–1 Forwarder

TRUMAN, HANBURY, BUXTON

MASTERS OF THE ROAD

Trucks have been used for carrying goods since the turn of the century. These early trucks (*above*), however, are a far cry from today's giant long-haul trucks (*above top*), many of which pull huge loads in excess of 48 tonnes. Their turbo-charged diesel engines are often monitored by computers to achieve maximum performance. These trucks are now the main land cargo-carriers.

AUTOBAHN TO MOTORWAY

Modern motorways, with their complex 'spaghetti' junctions (*left*), have their origins in the wide, two-lane 'autobahns' built in Germany in the 1930s. The US completed its first road that stretched right across the continent, the Lincoln Highway, in 1930. As car ownership grew in the US in the 1950s, a network of interstate motorways – 'freeways' – were built across the country.

THOMSON

ROBERT THOMSON (1822-73)

Thomson's ambition was to be a clergyman, until he changed his mind and became a successful engineer. He helped to build railways and invented the fountain pen. In 1845 he invented an inflatable rubber tyre. Although it was successful it was thought to be too expensive for general use.

GETTING OUT OF A JAM

The invention of the wheel is not all good news. As early as the 1920s, traffic jams have been common (*right*). City roads were unable to cope with the rapid growth of traffic. Many drivers now avoid making unnecessary journeys. Increasing numbers of people work from a home office, so they do not need to travel into work, while other people use bicycles or public transport.

MOTOR CARS

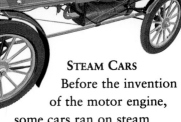

The first petrol-driven motor cars were made possible by the invention of the internal-combustion engine in 1863. 100 years later there are more than 95 million cars in the world. The internal-combustion engine, powered by coal-gas and air, was more compact and powerful than the steam engines that had been used previously. The first motor cars, produced during the 1880s by a German engineer, Karl Benz, were known as 'horseless carriages' (*left*). Some were little more than petrol-driven tricycles!

US-built 'horseless carriage' (1906)

STEAM CARS
Before the invention of the motor engine, some cars ran on steam (*above*). Such machines were restricted at first to a speed limit of 6.5 km/h (4 mph), later raised to 22.5 km/h (14 mph).

Delahaye type-135 (1936)

CARS FOR EVERYONE
In the 1930s, cars – such as the Delahaye type-135 (*above*) – were hand-made by skilled craftsmen, and cost more than £1,000, then a huge sum of money. Cheaper, mass-produced cars were first made in the US by Henry Ford. German Volkswagen Beetles (*below*), designed in the 1930s and first built in 1945, were marketed as 'people's cars'. They paved the way for the small cars of today (*above left*).

HENRY FORD (1863-1947)
In 1896 Henry Ford built his first car, the Quadricycle, mostly out of bicycle parts. His ambition was to build cars that everyone could afford. He set up an assembly line to build the famous 'Model T'. The firm he founded remains one of the world's most important companies.

FORD

HUMAN OR ROBOT HANDS

In 1913, Henry Ford introduced the moving assembly line (*below*), in which workers add parts to the cars as they pass. Many parts of modern mass-production cars are assembled by robots (*right*). The exact specifications of new models are fed into computers to enable engineers to accurately programme the assembly-line robots.

Robotic arms 'spot-welding' a body shell.

JAPANESE SUCCESS

In the 1980s, Japan overtook Britain, Germany and the US in car production. Japan's success is partly due to efficient working methods in its factories and its investment in robotic welders, assemblers and painters. As fuel had become more expensive after the 1973 Arab-Israeli War, the Japanese sold millions of small cars that had the advantage of being cheap to run.

This is the **EDSEL**

"It acts the way it looks, but it doesn't cost that much"

EDSEL

New member of the Ford family of fine cars

The Edsel's eighteen elegantly styled models are priced through the range where most people buy

DRIVING INTO THE FUTURE

Cars in the future may be made from lightweight materials such as aluminium and carbon-fibre, which would make them more economical on fuel. Electric cars, which run off rechargeable batteries, are another alternative (although power stations would still be used to make electricity). Solar-powered cars (*right*) have also been road-tested – but they need plenty of sunlight in order to work.

THE GAS GUZZLERS

During the 1950s large, sleek American cars with tail fins, chrome and bright colours became popular (*above*). They were a sign of American wealth. Although they used a great deal of petrol, or gasolene, fuel was inexpensive in the 1950s.

BUSES

Before the advent of the railways in the early 19th century, wealthy travellers used stagecoaches to make long-distance journeys. Routes were divided into stages of about 24 kilometres (15 miles). At the end of each stage the horses were changed at an inn. Modern long-distance coaches continue this tradition when they stop at bus stations.

HIGHWAY ROBBERY

Stagecoach travellers were often held up and robbed by highwaymen (*above*). Armed guards tried to protect the coaches. The best known highwayman, Dick Turpin, was eventually caught and hanged for murder in 1739.

MODERN COACHES

Millions of people go on holiday or travel long distances on luxury coaches (*right*). Passengers can relax in reclining seats and enjoy video entertainment. They are equipped with air-conditioning and toilets.

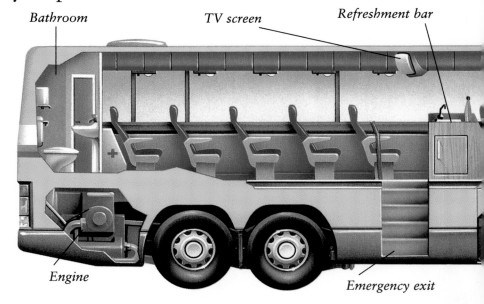

Bathroom

TV screen

Refreshment bar

Engine

Emergency exit

CITY BUSES

The first public bus service started in London in 1829. George Shillibeer, who owned them, called them omnibuses (*below*), although the public called them 'shillies' after him. London's streets were soon crowded with horse-drawn buses. Cities around the world also introduced buses. As towns grew in size and people moved out to the suburbs, bus services became even more indispensable. Articulated buses, with several sections (*above*), are now common in many European cities.

GEORGE SHILLIBEER
(1797-1866)
The first bus service was set up by George Shillibeer in London. Although buses later became popular, Shillibeer's business failed!

DAY TRIPPERS

After 1918 buses and coaches increasingly were used for long-distance journeys. Coach outings on single-decker coaches, called charabancs or 'chara' (below). were popular in the 1920s and 1930s. Longer journeys, to every part of Britain, were made by 'Royal Blue' coaches. Fares were cheaper than those on the railways.

TV screen

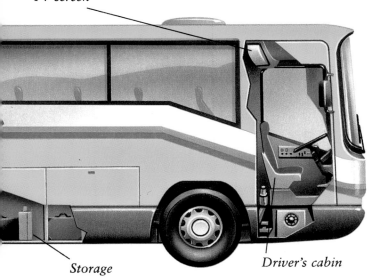

Storage

Driver's cabin

BUSES AT WAR

At the start of World War I (1914-18) the British Army was short of trucks. London buses were commandeered to move soldiers to the Front. When the German Army threatened to attack Paris these buses successfully rushed soldiers in to block their advance. It must have been a strange sight for the people of Paris – a fleet of red, double-decker London buses!

PERSONALISED BUSES

Decorated buses, often with religious ornaments (*above*), are common in the Himalayas and are a source of great pride to the families who own them.

INTERCITY COACHES

A network of 'Greyhound' and 'Trailways' long-distance buses (*below*) crisscrosses the US, linking cities and tourist attractions. In the 1940s and 1950s these buses carried millions of passengers. But gradually services declined as more people owned their own cars and air travel grew. In the US, however, as in Europe, long-distance buses are finding renewed favour with people as a cheaper alternative to going by rail or air.

NOT ENOUGH SEATS TO GO ROUND

Buses play an important role in countries where fewer people own cars. Many of the buses are uncomfortable, unsafe and overcrowded (*below*), but they provide a cheap and essential service. Buses and trains with people hanging on to the roof and sides is a common sight in places like India. The largest fleet of single-decker buses is in the city of São Paulo, Brazil, where there are more than 11,000 buses.

BICYCLES

Bicycles are one of the cheapest and simplest methods of travel. They are harmless to the environment and, once you get the hang of it, easy to ride. Early bicycles, which were

without pedals, were little more than toys. Later, in the 1860s, came the first pedal bicycles. People called them 'boneshakers' because they shook riders so violently. In the 1890s 'safety bicycles', with proper tyres and brakes, made a small revolution in transport. For the first time people had their own means of transport. Until the 1960s millions of people relied on bicycles to get to work.

'RUNNING MACHINES'
In 1817 Karl Drais, a German baron, produced a two-wheeled machine (*left*). Its two wheels were connected by a heavy bar with a saddle in the middle. Riders propelled it simply by pushing with their feet along the ground. It was known as a 'running machine'. English versions, called 'hobby horses', were popular among rich young men.

PENNY FARTHINGS
'Ordinary bicycles' of the 1870s were called penny farthings (*left*) because their wheels resembled two old British coins, the (big) penny and the (small) farthing.

HIGH-TECH BIKES

Modern high-tech bicycles are made of tough, lightweight materials. The most expensive racing bikes are made from aircraft-grade aluminium alloy with titanium gears.

Wheels are made from solid discs to reduce air resistance and riders wear streamlined polyester helmets. Mountain bikes (*left*), often with air-sprung shock-absorbers, are specially designed to race over steep and rough terrain. They are heavier than racing bikes.

GETTING INTO GEAR

Bike gears (*right*) make pedalling easier up or downhill. Sprung rollers move the chain onto different sprocket wheels. The chain turns faster on smaller sprocket wheels making going uphill easier.

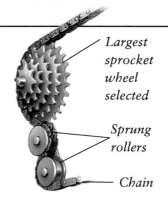

Largest sprocket wheel selected

Chain moves down a wheel

Sprung rollers

Chain

THE LOTUS BIKE
The frame of this high-tech racing bike (*left*) is made from a single piece of reinforced carbon fibre. The rear wheel is a flat disc, which decreases wind resistance.

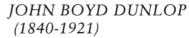

BOYD DUNLOP

JOHN BOYD DUNLOP (1840-1921)
Dunlop made the first successful pneumatic tyres for bicycles. A Scottish veterinarian, he made tyres out of rubber hose for his child's toy tricycle. This led him to set up the Dunlop Rubber Company to produce tyres for bicycles and, later, for cars.

KEEP CYCLING!
In countries where fewer people own cars, the bicycle is an important means of transport. In heavily populated places like China (*left*), masses of people depend on the bicycle as their only means of travel. Other countries, like Holland, are trying to encourage more people to use bikes to reduce pollution levels.

PEDAL TAXIS
Rickshaws are small, two- or three-wheeled, hooded carriages, pulled or pushed by a bicycle (*below*), or by a person. In many cities in Asia they form a cheap taxi service. Other types of rickshaw transport food and other goods to markets.

MOTORCYCLES

US Militaire (1914)

The first motorcycle was a wooden bicycle fitted with a petrol engine. Invented in 1885 by a German engineer called Gottlieb Daimler, it was only slightly faster than walking. By 1900 several firms were making motorcycles and, by 1914, America was taking the lead in technical development with bikes like the Militaire (*above*). Motorcycles were used by soldiers in wartime and are used by police officers and couriers today. But for many enthusiasts motorbikes are one of the most thrilling forms of transport in the world.

Knobbly tyres increase grip

Twin-engine Royal Enfield bike (1960)

Honda Super Blackbird

TWIN-ENGINES AND 'SUPERBIKES'

From the 1940s, bikes were built with twin-cylinder engines for improved performance (*above*). Modern 'superbikes' can perform as well as Formula-One racing cars. This Japanese Honda *Super Blackbird* (*right*) is the world's most powerful bike. Its top speed is 300 km/h (188 mph) and it can accelerate from 0-96 km/h (0-60 mph) in 2.5 seconds.

SCOOTER CRAZES

Scooters are an Italian invention, first produced by Vespa in 1947. These simple motorbikes are still popular with young people in Europe. In the 1960s scooters were favoured by teenagers called 'mods'. Some of them embellished their scooters with extra lights and mirrors (*left*). These 'mod' bikes are now valuable collectors' items.

BIKE SAFETY

Safety is now an important issue in motorbike manufacturing. Designers make handling easier by improving suspension and steering systems. Some of the most expensive bikes use air-sprung shock-absorbers to reduce the impact of bumps.

HARLEY-DAVIDSON

The famous American 'Harleys' are ridden by the US Army, most US police forces and thousands of other people – including the notorious 'Hells Angels' (*left*). The first Harley bike was built in 1907. In 1965 it introduced the Electra Glide – one of the most luxurious motorcycles ever produced. Recent models have a five-speed gearbox, disc brakes and a rubber-mounted engine. The firm is one of the few US makes to survive competition from Japanese manufacturers today.

GOTTLIEB DAIMLER
(1834-1900)
Daimler, a German engineer and inventor, is most famous for his motor cars. But he built the very first motorcycle before he built cars. His motorcycle was made mostly out of wood and his son Paul rode 9.5 kms (6 miles) on it to become the first motorcyclist.

MOTORCYCLE POLICE
Motorcycles are vital to the police (*left*). Motorcycle outriders escort ambulances and important people such as prime ministers and presidents.

SEATED SIDE BY SIDE

During World War II (1939-45) Germany fitted motorcycles and sidecars with machine guns, while Britain and America used bikes mainly for staff work (*above*). After the war, sidecars were used before motorcars became widely affordable. Sidecars are now made in smaller numbers, and high-tech ones can cost as much as motor cars; this model, made in Germany, costs £34,000 (*right*)!

FARMING QUADS
Quads are motorcycles with four large wheels used for riding across rough terrain (*right*). They are useful for farmers but many people also enjoy the excitement of cross-country racing.

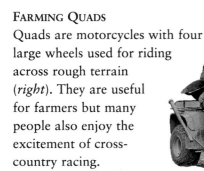

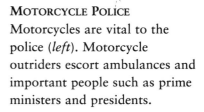

RAILWAYS

The first steam-powered trains were built in the early 1800s by Richard Trevithick in England and Oliver Evans in the US. In 1830, George and Robert Stephenson's *Rocket* managed a speed of 32 km/h (20 mph). At first people thought that the force of such speeds would harm passengers! The railways, however, expanded rapidly over the 19th century and brought far-away places closer.

EARLY RAILWAYS
Before steam locomotives, horses were used to pull trucks along short railway lines linking coal mines to canals and ports (*above*).

SIGNALLING
In the early days of the railways, signals were given by flags (*above*).

'Gladstone' (1880s)

Mallard

MALLARD

ICE

CITY RAILWAYS

COAST TO COAST
Railways were vital to the expansion of the US in the 19th century. Some US steam trains had 'cow catchers' on the front (*below*) to reduce the impact of collisions.

As cities grew in size at the start of the 20th century, new forms of rail transport were developed. Electric trains are well-suited to urban areas: they can stop and start quickly; they are quiet and, unlike steam trains, they produce no soot. The world's first public electric railway was opened in Germany in 1881. To avoid congestion, some urban trains run underground or, like the automated, driverless trains of the Docklands Light Railway in London (*above*), travel overhead.

STATION TO STATION

The Victorians were thrilled with the railways. By 1900 more than 30,000 kilometres (18,641 miles) of railway line had been built in Britain alone. The US now has over 320,000 kilometres (200,000 miles).

Cathedral-like railway stations (*right*) were built in many cities. Waterloo-International (*below*) is a spacious new station in London that services the Eurostar trains that run through the Channel Tunnel to France.

HIGH-SPEED TRAINS (*BELOW LEFT*)
The first steam trains travelled at a horse's pace but, by the end of the 19th century, some trains reached 160 km/h (100mph). The fastest steam train is *Mallard*, which reached 202 km/h (126 mph) in 1938. Modern high-speed trains, like Germany's Inter-city Express (ICE) and France's TGV, travel at 300 km/h (186 mph).

ORIENT EXPRESS
The world's most luxurious train, the *Orient Express*, ran from Paris to Istanbul in the early 20th century. It began running again in the 1980s (*above*).

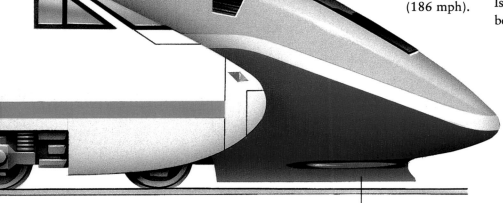

TGV

STEPHENSON

FREIGHT TRAINS

The development of train travel meant that fresh food could be transported cheaply into cities. Lengthy freight trains are common in the US and Canada (*below*) where the huge distances make rail freight economical. The longest freight train, which ran in South Africa, had 660 wagons, 16 locomotives, and was 7.3 kilometres (4.5 miles) long!

GEORGE STEPHENSON (1781-1848)
Called 'the father of the railways', Stephenson was a self-educated engineer whose Rocket (above) won a competition in the north of England for the best locomotive. He helped to prove that railways could be successful. He also showed how railway lines could be built almost anywhere.

TRAMS

During the 1830s the first horse-drawn trams (*right*) – called streetcars or trolley cars – appeared in US cities.

In Britain trams appeared during the 1860s. At first, they were used mainly by factory workers. Electric trams are powered by electricity from overhead cables and run on rails embedded in roads. For city dwellers, they were a faster and cheaper alternative to horse-drawn buses.

EUROPEAN TRAMS
In cities like Vienna, Austria, and Stuttgart, Germany, trams with linked carriages (*above*) are more common than buses.

ELECTRIC POWER
The first trams and trolley buses to be supplied with electric power from overhead cables appeared in the 1880s (*above*). They were – and still are – one of the best ways to get around in towns.

CABLE CARS
The famous cable cars, or grip cars, began running in San Francisco in 1873. They are still running today (*below*).

WERNER VON SIEMENS (1816-92)
A German engineer, von Siemens developed the electric telegraph system. Messages were sent along cables using electricity. From that he worked out how power cables could be set high up along streets and safely supply electricity to trams. His invention was important long before motor buses were in use.

VON SIEMENS

RETURN OF THE TRAM

During the 1940s and 1950s many tramways in Europe and the US were replaced by bus services. But, as trams cost less to run than buses, cause less pollution in cities and can carry more passengers (by using several carriages), new tramway systems are now being built. Light Rapid Transit railways (*right*) are a cross between trams and trains.

SUBWAYS

The world's first underground railway opened in London in 1863, followed by one in New York in 1904. By 1930 New York had 358 kilometres (224 miles) of subway line. At first, trains were pulled by steam locomotives which made tunnels and stations sooty and inhospitable. Early subways were usually shallow, brick-lined trenches with a roof. Today, they are built much deeper down. Subways form an essential part of densely populated cities.

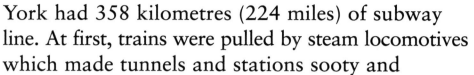

NEW LINES
The 19th-century British Prime Minister, Gladstone, sitting on the far left, attends the opening of a new line of the London underground (*left*).

TYPES OF TRAIN
Electric trains have a third 'live' rail running between the two outside rails (*right*). In Paris, the metro trains use wheels with rubber rims – this makes them much quieter.

'Live' rail

RUSH HOUR!

Staff on the Tokyo subway in Japan squeeze in as many passengers as possible during the rush hour (*left*). But the busiest underground is in the Russian capital city, Moscow. It transports more than three billion passengers a year. New York City has the most underground stations – 468!

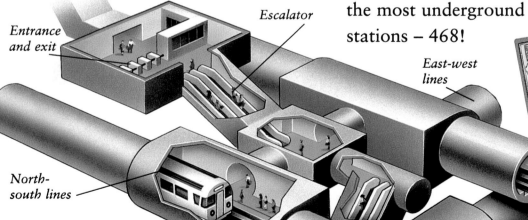

Entrance and exit

Escalator

East-west lines

North-south lines

Rail tunnels are built on different levels so they pass over or under each other; passenger tunnels and escalators connect the platforms.

ON THE MAP
As cities grew, subways were extended. By the 1930s Londoners could go for a day out in the countryside (*above*). Many people moved to the suburbs.

CANALS, BRIDGES & TUNNELS

All forms of transport are faced with natural obstacles, and engineers have had to find ways of overcoming them. The ancient Greeks built canals across land as shortcuts for ships and the Romans invented aqueducts – bridges that carried water across valleys. The Romans also coined the word 'engineer' from the Latin word *ingenium*, meaning genius. Modern engineering began in the 18th century with the Industrial Revolution. New materials such as iron and steel began to replace stone and brick. The first bridge built entirely of iron (*right*) was finished in 1780 at Ironbridge, England.

EARLY CANALS
The ancient Egyptians (*above*) built canals to irrigate crops in areas that received very little water. Their knowledge of canal-building spread throughout the Middle East to Europe.

towpath

CANAL BOATS
Before boats were fitted with engines, they were towed by horses, who walked alongside on paths known as 'towpaths' (*above*). Until the railways, canals were vital for the transport of heavy and fragile goods.

CANALS FOR CARGO

Canals and rivers carry huge barges carrying thousands of tonnes of cargo – an inland country such as Switzerland relies on the River Rhine to take goods through Germany to the sea. Some canals were originally used to transport raw materials like coal, and are now used mostly for canal-boat holidays.

THE SUEZ CANAL
The 184-km (114-mile) long Suez Canal (*below*), opened in 1869, cuts through Egypt to link the Mediterranean Sea with the Red Sea. This great feat of engineering took ten years to build. It cut thousands of kilometres off the trip from India and the Far East to Europe. Today it is a vital route for oil tankers.

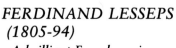

FERDINAND LESSEPS (1805-94)

A brilliant French engineer, Lesseps forwarded the idea of the Suez Canal after visiting Egypt. On its completion he was acclaimed as a great hero.

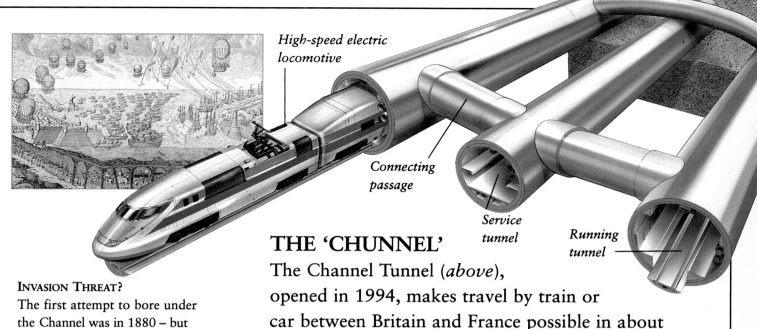

High-speed electric locomotive

Connecting passage

Service tunnel

Running tunnel

THE 'CHUNNEL'

The Channel Tunnel (*above*), opened in 1994, makes travel by train or car between Britain and France possible in about 30 minutes. The tunnel is 50 kilometres (30 miles) long – just four kilometres (3.5 miles) shorter than the longest tunnel in the world, at Seikan in Japan.

INVASION THREAT?
The first attempt to bore under the Channel was in 1880 – but progress was halted because of the supposed threat to British defences (*above top*)!

TOWER BRIDGE
Tower Bridge, London (*left*), is a famous example of a bascule bridge – one in which the bridge tilts upwards to let ships pass. Cars drive across when the bridge is down.

FROM LOGS TO SUSPENSION

The first bridges were made of pieces of wood laid across streams. As road travel and railways increased, bridge building improved. The longest bridges – suspension bridges, such as this one in Normandy, France (*right*) – are held in place by cables supported by towers at each end. San Francisco's Golden Gate Bridge, opened in 1937, has a span of 1,280 metres (4,200 feet).

BUILDING BRIDGES
Long bridges are built in stages (*left*). The weight of each section is supported by intermediate piers crowned with towers, from which parallel cables are suspended.

ROADS

The first roads were tracks used by people and animals. The earliest paved roads were built in Mesopotamia (now Iraq) in 2200 BC. From 1200 to 1500 AD, the Incas in South America built a huge network of roads linking their cities. Many modern roads in Europe follow the routes of old Roman roads.

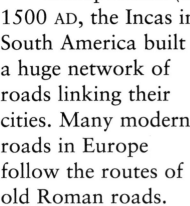

ROMAN ROADS
The Romans were the first great road builders (*above*). Their roads had firm foundations and paved surface that were not worn away by marching soldiers or horses.

TURNPIKES
In the 18th century, travellers in England paid to use certain roads at gates called turnpikes (*left*). Tolls are still paid on some motorways in Europe and the US – they help pay for repairs.

ROAD-LAYING MACHINES
Motorways are built by huge machines (*above*), which perform several functions. A concrete mixer in front pours concrete over the road base. A levelling machine and smoothing machine follow.

MIGHTY MOTORWAYS

Motorways (*below*), which cost around £6 million per kilometre to build, need solid foundations and non-skid surfaces. Slightly curved surfaces, called cambers, let rainwater drain off. Some modern roads are made up of slabs of concrete joined by bitumen, or tar. Because roads undergo constant wear and tear, they have to be resurfaced frequently, sometimes as often as every three years or so.

JOHN McADAM (1756-1836)
Modern roads are surfaced with a mixture of tar and small stones called 'tarmac', or 'tarmacadam'. It was the idea of John McAdam, a Scotsman, who had the job of repairing the busy London to Bristol turnpike road in the early 1800s.

McADAM

RAILS

Rails were used in Europe several centuries before the first steam trains. They made the wheels of carts run more easily. The first iron railways had raised edges, called flanges, which held wheels on the line. Later, flanges were taken off rails and put on wheels. Some modern high-speed trains, such as the 'bullet' trains in Japan, need specially fitted tracks.

RUTTED ROADS
The earliest type of track used stone or timber placed in ruts worn by cart wheels. The Romans used these rutted roads (*above*) to guide carts.

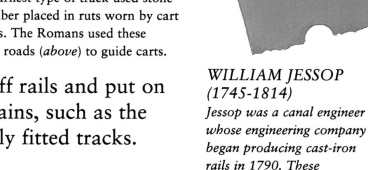

WILLIAM JESSOP (1745-1814)
Jessop was a canal engineer whose engineering company began producing cast-iron rails in 1790. These cheap, strong rails were an important advance in railway track technology.

MODERN TRACK

The first wooden rails were used at coalfields in the mid-16th century (*right*). Horses could pull much heavier loads if their carts ran on rails. Wooden rails tended to crack

and split, however, so iron plates were laid over them. After 1760, cast-iron rails began to replace wooden tracks, and a century later much stronger rails made of steel became common.

BATTLE OF THE GAUGES
The gauge is the width between the rails. Countries around the world have different gauges. In Britain, there was a conflict between the great railway builders, George Stephenson and Isambard Brunel. Eventually the government sided with Stephenson. His gauge is still the standard width of British railways.

MOUNTAIN RAILS
In some mountainous areas railways have an extra toothed rail. Carriages are fitted with cogwheels which grip the teeth as they climb very steep slopes (*above*).

MONORAIL SYSTEMS *have only one rail, from which the train is hung.*

THE ALWEG SYSTEM *uses three or four supporting wheels to reduce friction.*

MAGLEV TRAINS *do not use rails. Powerful magnets cause the train to 'float'.*

CARGO SHIPS

About 70 percent of the earth's surface is covered with water. Ships and boats are the oldest form of transport, first developed by the ancient Egyptians. For thousands of years ships have played a vital part in trade. Today, ships carry more than three quarters of the world's international cargo.

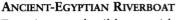

ANCIENT-EGYPTIAN RIVERBOAT
Egyptians used sail boats with square sails on the River Nile (*above*) as early as 3000 BC.

VIKING SHIPS
Over 1,000 years ago Vikings from northern Europe sailed in warships called longboats (*left*). Their boats were 20-25 m (66-82 ft) long and carried 40 men. The bravest crews sailed across the Atlantic Ocean to Greenland and America.

CARGO SHIPS

Today, giant container ships (*right*) transport huge cargoes across the oceans. The containers are loaded and unloaded by cranes. Some loose cargoes, such as grain, coal and metal ores, are poured straight into bulk carriers, which have specially divided holds. The largest cargo ship is an oil tanker, the *Jahre Viking*. It weighs 564,763 tonnes and is 458 metres (1,502 feet) long. Europe's long-established shipbuilding industry has declined and most new ships are built in Japan or Korea.

GIANTS OF THE SEA
Oil tankers (*right*) carry vital oil supplies from the Middle East to Europe, the US and Japan.

ROMAN MERCHANT SHIPS
Merchant ships (*above*) sailed from Italy to all parts of the Roman Empire. They carried supplies of weapons, wine and equipment for overseas soldiers.

CUSHIONED BY AIR

Hovercraft (*right*) are ships that travel over sea or land on a layer of compressed air. This 'cushion' of air reduces friction so they can travel at speeds of up to 130 km/h (81 mph). Hovercraft transport freight, vehicles and people.

NAVIGATION METHODS

Early navigators used the Sun and stars to work out their position at sea. By 200 BC instruments called astrolabes (*left*) were used to measure the exact positions of bright stars. The ancient Chinese were the first to discover magnets, which were found to always point north. Radar was introduced in the 1930s to detect ships in fog, and communication satellites (*right*) are now used to fix exact positions.

SAIL-ASSISTED SHIPS

Some modern high-tech ships are equipped with sails (*below*). But these sails are nothing like those on old sailing ships. They are computer controlled to catch the wind. Combined with engine power, the use of sails can reduce a ship's fuel bill by ten percent.

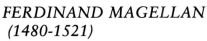

FERDINAND MAGELLAN (1480-1521)

Magellan, a Portuguese navigator, set off to sail around the world in 1519. He travelled around the stormy foot of South America into a calm ocean, which he named the 'Pacific'. Magellan was killed by natives in the Philippines.

PASSENGER LINERS

Before air travel, the only way to cross an ocean was by ship. Passenger travel became popular in the early 19th century when the first steamships were introduced. During the late 19th and early 20th centuries, millions of people sailed from Europe to North America or Australia to emigrate. Sea travel declined in the early 1960s, when most people began to travel by aeroplane. Now, many people take cruises in luxury liners.

THE FIRST LIGHTHOUSE
The famous Lighthouse of Alexandria, Egypt, guided ships into the city's harbour for 1,500 years before an earthquake destroyed it in the 14th century AD.

CRUISING

The era of great ocean liners began in the 1840s with the SS *Great Britain* (*below*), the first iron-hulled steamship to cross the Atlantic. During the 1930s travelling by ocean liner was glamorous and luxurious. Today this tradition is carried on by cruise liners. Passengers expect top facilities and entertainment. Cruise ships have swimming pools, theatres, casinos and restaurants. Some of the most popular trips are around the Caribbean, through the Panama Canal or along the coast of Alaska.

Cabins

THE *TITANIC*
In 1912 the 'unsinkable' liner SS *Titanic* (*left*) sank after hitting an iceberg. There were too few lifeboats and only 700 people were saved, while 1,500 lives were lost.

BRUNEL

ISAMBARD BRUNEL (1806-59)
Brunel was a shipbuilder, whose methods were copied by later engineers. In 1837 his Great Western was the first steamship to start a regular passenger service across the Atlantic.

QUEEN OF CRUISERS

The *Carnival Destiny* (*below*) is the biggest cruise ship in the world. It is 241 m (791 ft) long, weighs 101,000 tons and is taller than the Statue of Liberty – 56 m (184 ft).

A central area towers up nine decks to a glass dome.

MISSISSIPPI RIVER BOAT

Steam engines turn a huge paddle wheel at the stern, or back, of river boats on the Mississippi River in the US (*right*). In the 1800s, hundreds of these craft transported cotton and passengers to and from New Orleans. Today they are tourist attractions.

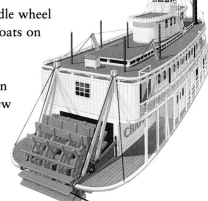

Paddle wheel

Theatre

Hydrofoil's single pair of wings

LIFE JACKETS
Early life jackets (*left*) were filled with cork to keep people afloat. Modern inflatable life jackets are designed to leave the arms free while keeping the head and shoulders above water in case the wearer is unconscious (*below*).

They are usually bright orange and have a whistle to attract attention. Every ship is obliged to carry enough life jackets – and lifeboats – for all passengers and crew.

MODERN BOATS

Traditional ferries are being replaced by huge new high-speed ferries. Hydrofoils, too, are common: a pair of 'wings' under the hulls lifts them out of the water (*above*), causing less 'drag', so greater speeds can be reached than with conventional boats. Twin-hulled catamarans (*right*) can reach speeds of 40 knots using 100,000 horsepower engines.

RACING TO VICTORY

Many forms of transport are used for sport and leisure. While some people go cycling, canoeing or ballooning for pleasure, sports people test their skill and stamina by competing against each other to set up new records. These sports are also a test of machines. Manufacturers and designers compete to produce faster, more efficient vehicles: the racing cars of 1914 (*right*) look a bit like toys compared to today's sleek, aerodynamic cars (*below right*).

SPEED ON THE WATER

Yachting is a popular recreation as well as a sport. It started in the Netherlands (the word 'yacht' comes from the Dutch 'jacht' meaning small vessel). By 1900 (*above*), yachting was popular worldwide. The America's Cup (*below*) was first raced in 1851. US yachts won the trophy consistently until 1983, when an Australian boat won.

SURF'S UP!
Windsurfing (*above*) is an energetic sport with speeds of over 84 km/h (52 mph) – and it does not cause any air pollution!

DAMON HILL (1960-)
Damon Hill, who won the 1996 World Motor Racing Championship, has followed in his father's footsteps. Graham Hill twice won the championship in the 1960s.

PUSHING THE BOAT OUT

Competitive rowing began in the 1700s and was accepted as an Olympic sport in 1900. Rowing

races, called regattas, are held annually in many

parts of the world. Most boats have four or eight oars, each rowed by one person, but single-person sculls (where one rower uses two oars) are also used (*left*).

THE BOAT RACE
The most famous annual boat race, between Oxford and Cambridge universities (*above*), first took place in 1829. It is raced over a 6-km 780-m (4.2-mile) stretch of the River Thames and lasts about 20 minutes.

FORMULA ONE
The most important motor races are the Formula-One Grand-Prix races which are held all over the world. These races feature the fastest racing cars driven by the most skilled drivers. Some cars (*left*) reach speeds of 340 km/h (213 mph).

These cyclists (right) lead the 1930 Tour de France.

TOUR DE FRANCE

LAND-SPEED RECORDS
The 1.6-km (1-mile) land-speed record increased from 205.447 km/h (127.659 mph) in 1906 to 1019.7 km/h (633.6 mph) in 1983. American Al Teague holds the record for the fastest wheel-driven car (*below*) – 696.331 km/h (432.692 mph).

Organised cycle racing began in France in 1868. The greatest race of all is the annual Tour de France, which was first run in 1903. For three weeks riders race for 5,000 km (3,000 miles) along a gruelling route that includes a climb into the French Alps. At the start of each stage the overall leader is given a yellow jersey to wear (*right*).

ANIMAL POWER

For thousands of years animals have been used to carry people and goods, or to pull vehicles. Dogs – the first domesticated animals – were probably the first animals used to pull vehicles. They pulled the simple wooden sleds of travelling nomads who lived in central Asia and, in some places, dogs have pulled small carts (this was banned in Britain in 1834). In many countries the use of animals is still very important.

HANNIBAL'S ELEPHANTS
In 218 BC, Hannibal, a general from north Africa, moved his troops through the Alps using elephants (*above*) and mounted a surprise attack on the Roman army.

BEASTS OF BURDEN

For centuries elephants (*above*) have been used to transport heavy equipment and to move heavy trees in rainforests. Camels (*below*) make excellent beasts of burden in hot, dry countries. They can survive for many months without water or food and, with their two-toed feet, they are sure-footed on rocks and sand. For thousands of years camels have been used to carry goods and pull carts and passenger coaches. Processions of camels, called camel trains, travelled along the Silk Road. This ancient trade route linked Europe with China when Chinese silk was in great demand in Europe. In North Africa today camels are still used to transport goods and people.

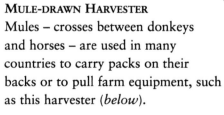

MULE-DRAWN HARVESTER
Mules – crosses between donkeys and horses – are used in many countries to carry packs on their backs or to pull farm equipment, such as this harvester (*below*).

EGYPTIAN DONKEYS

Thousands of years ago the ancient Egyptians used donkeys with packs on their backs (*left*). Donkeys need less water than horses and were common in many parts of Africa, where rainfall is slight. Many poor people all over the world still use donkey power.

THE HORSE

Modern horses descended from three separate types that emerged after the last Ice Age (10,000 years ago). Saddles, harnesses and training methods have been developed over centuries of use, making the horse the most versatile of all working animals.

HORSE

HARD-WORKING HUSKIES

Inuit Eskimos, who live in the far north of Canada, traditionally rely on husky dogs to pull their sleds across the snow. Today, husky dogs are more commonly used to carry around tourists (*below*)!

Brewery dray

HORSE POWER

All types of motor vehicles were originally horse-drawn, including ambulances and buses. Even today horses are used by some breweries to pull low, strong carts called drays (*left*).

Early American settlers crossed the Great Plains in horse-drawn wagons called prairie schooners

(*below left*). They formed wagon trains to support each other on the long journey.

SACRED COWS

In many Asian countries, cows are valuable animals, used to pull heavy ploughs (*left*) which break up the hard soil in the fields. In India, the main religion, Hinduism, treats cows with reverence and forbids anyone to kill them.

They also provide many essentials of the Indian diet such as milk and butter. The dried dung is even used as a form of fuel!

GLOSSARY

Articulated buses Buses that are made in sections linked by a flexible joint.

Assembly line A manufacturing method in which workers are positioned in lines and pass on the work from stage to stage.

Autobahn The name given to German motorways. The first autobahns were built in the 1930s by Adolf Hitler's government to speed up the movement of troops and equipment.

Bicycles Two-wheeled vehicles that became popular in the 19th century. They are still a common form of transport

today, particularly in developing countries.

Bulk carriers Vessels that carry cargo, such as grain, that is not in the form of separate packages.

Bullet trains Streamlined, very fast trains that have been used on Japanese railways since 1964. Bullet trains can reach speeds of 210 km/h (130 mph).

Buses Known in full as 'omnibuses', buses are passenger-carrying vehicles that were originally pulled by horses and are now engine-powered.

Canals Canals are artificial waterways built to connect inland places with rivers or seas. They allow heavy loads to be carried more easily than by road. Since the building of railways, they have declined in importance.

Catamarans Sail boats fitted with twin hulls. The design is based on rafts used on the St Lawrence River in Canada. These rafts are made of two boats positioned side by side.

Charabancs Long single-decker tourist coaches popular in the 1920s and 1930s. They are named after the French word for 'carriage with benches' (*char-à-banc*).

Commercial vehicles General term for vehicles that carry goods, such as lorries and trucks, and buses and coaches, which carry passengers.

Engineer Someone who designs or makes engines, machinery or public works such as roads, railways, bridges and canals.

Environment The condition of our surroundings. People are increasingly concerned about the impact of transport systems on the environment.

Friction The force produced when two moving objects rub against each other. Also known as 'drag', this force slows down moving objects.

Gauge The width between the rails of railway lines.

Grand Prix Any of several international motor races; any competition of similar importance in other sports

Horsepower Originally the power a horse can exert, now used as a measure of an engine's power.

Hull The frame or body of a ship.

Hydrofoils Ships that rise above the water as they reach high speeds. The first successful hydrofoil was built in Italy in 1906 but they did not come into general use until the 1950s.

Industrial Revolution The period from about 1760 when factories began to use power-driven machinery. Before this, industry was carried out by people at home using simple machinery.

Internal-combustion engine An engine in which the fuel is burned within cylinders in order to drive a piston. Steam engines, which were employed before the invention of the internal-combustion engine, use external combustion, which is less efficient.

Knot The unit of speed for ships, a knot is equal to 1.85 km (one nautical mile) per hour. In the early days of sailing, knots were tied on a line which was then released into the sea as a ship sailed in order to measure its speed.

LRT (Light Rapid Transit) These modern railways, which are a cross between trams and trains, provide a good form of transport in cities.

Maglev Railways that use magnetic levitation as propulsion. They were first used in 1984 at Birmingham Airport, England.

Middle Ages (AD 500 – 1500) The historical period in Europe between ancient and modern times.

It extends from the fall of the Roman Empire to the rebirth of arts and architecture in Italy, known as the Renaissance.

Monorail Trains that travel on a single rail.

Motor cars Vehicles powered by diesel, petrol or electric engines. The first cars were built in the 1880s.

Motorcycles Two-wheeled vehicles having one or two saddles. An unsuccessful steam-powered bicycle was invented in France in 1868; the first petrol-driven bikes were made in Germany in the 1880s.

Motorways Roads with at least two lanes in each direction intended to allow

vehicles to travel at greater speeds.

Mountain bicycles Bicycles with strong, heavy frames and wide tyres designed for use over bumpy surfaces.

Navigation The method of finding a spacial position and following a route. Originally, geometry and the position of the stars were used to plot courses.

Ocean liners Large, comfortable ships that are used to carry passengers on long journeys. They have been replaced by air travel but are still used for holiday cruises.

Propellers Screw-type devices used to propel ships and aircraft. The first large ship to use a screw propeller was the SS *Great Britain,* designed in 1845 by the British engineer Isambard Brunel.

Radar Equipment which sends and receives high-powered radio pulses which bounce off objects or people to locate their position.

Railways The success of public railways in Britain after 1830 led to the building of railways all over the world.

Rickshaws Light two- or three-wheeled people-powered taxis first used in Japan in the 1870s.

Roman Empire At its height in the AD 100s, the Roman Empire covered about half of Europe, much of the Middle East, and the north coast of Africa.

Safety bicycles The first 'modern' type of bicycle, first used in 1885. The pedals are linked by the chain to the centre of the rear wheel.

Satellites Spacecraft that orbit the earth and send back radio signals which are used by ships to fix their positions.

Stagecoaches Horse-drawn coaches used for carrying passengers and post before the railways were built.

Suburbs The outskirts of cities.

Subway Another name for underground railways. Cities with underground railways include London, New York, Los Angeles, Paris, Prague and Moscow.

Superbikes Motorbikes which are designed and built to have the best possible performance.

Suspension bridges Bridges in which the roadway is suspended from ropes or cables between towers built of steel or masonry.

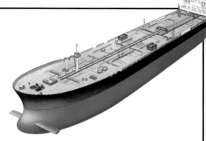

TGV (**Train á Grande Vitesse**) French high-speed trains that travel on specially designed rails. The TGV began operating in 1981.

Trams Passenger vehicles that run on tracks laid along the road and are powered by electricity from overhead cables. Many tram services had been ended by the 1950s but they are being revived because they are environmentally friendly and efficient.

Trucks Heavy vehicles, also called lorries, used to carry goods. The most powerful trucks pull a number of huge trailors.

Tricycles Cycles with three wheels. Young children often ride tricycles because they are more stable than bicycles.

Turnpikes Roads, usually fast, main roads, on which tolls are paid by passengers in order to contribute to their upkeep.

INDEX

Picture Credits
(t=top, m=middle, c=centre, b=bottom, r=right, l=left):
front cover tlt, tm & mc, 4m, 7mr, 8t, 13mb, 14t, 16tr, 17t & b, 19t, 27m, 28b, 31mr & back cover – Mary Evans Picture Library; front cover tlb, 5t & 23b – Solution Pictures; front cover trt – Hoverspeed; front cover trb & mlb – AKG London; front cover mlt – Renault UK; front cover mr, 3, 9br, 10b, 11m, 13t & bl, 14b, 15ml & mr, 16bl, 18b, 19br, 20b, 21, 22-23, 25br, 26bl & br, 27bl & br, 28m, 28-29 & 29b – Frank Spooner Pictures; front cover b – Fodden/Paccar Trucks; 4-5, 9bl & 28t – Hutchinson Picture Library; 5b, 7ml, 9t, 10m, 12 both, 15t, 16m, 20mr, 24 & 26t – Hulton Getty Collection; 6m & 7t – Ford UK; 8m, 9m, 15b & 25bl – Eye Ubiquitous; 10-11, 11b, 13mt, 16br, 17m, 18m, 19bl, 26-27 & 29t – Rex Features; 12-13 – Honda UK; 13br – The World Motorcycle News Agency; 16tl – NMVB; 19m – Roger Vlitos; 20ml – Balfour Beatty; 23t – Charles de Vere